Routledge Revivals

I0025217

Before the Bluestockings

First published in 1929, *Before the Bluestockings* is a study of the individual lives and the position of educated Englishwomen from the Restoration to the end of the first third of the eighteenth century. The question is approached not only from the women's point of view—Hannah Woolley, Mary Astell and Elizabeth Elstob—but also records the views of contemporary observers like Lord Halifax, John Locke, George Ballard and Sir Richard Steele.

Before the Bluestockings

Ada Wallas

Routledge
Taylor & Francis Group

First published in 1929
by George Allen & Unwin Ltd.

This edition first published in 2024 by Routledge
4 Park Square, Milton Park, Abingdon, Oxon, OX14 4RN

and by Routledge
605 Third Avenue, New York, NY 10017

Routledge is an imprint of the Taylor & Francis Group, an informa business

© 1929 Ada Wallas

All rights reserved. No part of this book may be reprinted or reproduced or utilised in any form or by any electronic, mechanical, or other means, now known or hereafter invented, including photocopying and recording, or in any information storage or retrieval system, without permission in writing from the publishers.

Publisher's Note
The publisher has gone to great lengths to ensure the quality of this reprint but points out that some imperfections in the original copies may be apparent.

Disclaimer
The publisher has made every effort to trace copyright holders and welcomes correspondence from those they have been unable to contact.

A Library of Congress record exists under LCCN: 29027651

ISBN: 978-1-032-90744-4 (hbk)
ISBN: 978-1-003-55959-7 (ebk)
ISBN: 978-1-032-90745-1 (pbk)

Book DOI 10.4324/9781003559597

A Serious
PROPOSAL
To the
Ladies,

For the Advancement of
their true and greatest
Interest.

By a Lover of Her SEX.

LONDON,
Printed for R. Wilkin at
the King's Head in St. Paul's
Church-Yard. 1694.

*For the Honourable
M^r. Mountague.*

from her Ladiships

Most humble Servant

M. A.

TITLE PAGE OF MARY ASTELL'S "SERIOUS PROPOSAL", 1694, AND DEDICATION IN
THE AUTHORESS'S HAND

Before the Bluestockings

by

Ada Wallas

(*Mrs. Graham Wallas*)

TO

G. W.

C. W.

THESE six essays are the result of an attempt to understand, mainly by the study of individual lives, the position of educated Englishwomen from the Restoration to the end of the first third of the eighteenth century. The question is approached from the point of view, not only of the women themselves, but also of such contemporary observers as Lord Halifax, John Locke, George Ballard and Sir Richard Steele.

I have chosen my title in order to indicate a distinction between these women, who were conscious of intellectual needs and powers, but received little or no general recognition, and the "Bluestockings" (Mrs. Montagu, Mrs. Carter, Mrs. Vesey and their friends) who, a generation later, owed their position in Society to their reputation for learning.

Chapters II and IV have already appeared in *The Contemporary Review*.

I have to thank my nephew, Mr. A. E. Popham of the British Museum, for help in selecting the illustrations.

A. W.

CONTENTS

ILLUSTRATIONS

HANNAH WOOLLEY

CHAPTER I

HANNAH WOOLLEY

A Self-supporting Woman of the Seventeenth Century

THE material position of a young English gentlewoman whose father owned land in the seventeenth century was fairly secure. Though her education was often left to chance, her parents always did their best to arrange a marriage for her, by which she should be maintained in comfort, and which at the same time should add to their own wealth and importance.

But there were other young gentlewomen, the portionless and often penniless daughters of younger sons who had no estate, or of men who, in the rapidly changing political and religious fortunes of the country, had forfeited lands, money, and posts. They had to support themselves by work, and the only kind of work open to them was some form of service in the house of a lady of quality. Even in the reign of Victoria, girls in this position were generally unfitted by want of training for any employment better than that of an overworked and ill-paid governess. But the poor gentlewomen of the seventeenth century could not as a rule become teachers, owing to the crude fact—to which so many writers of the time bear testimony—that it was unusual for them to be able

B

to read or write with ease. The position of a young man from such a family was bad enough; but he would have been sent to some kind of school, and by a stroke of the pen a patron could secure him a university scholarship or a living. His sister had no choice but service. There were, it is true, grades in service; by favour or unusual exertions a clever girl might become the "waiting woman", or even the stewardess, of some great lady; but more often she had to accept menial work as a chamber- or scullery-maid. Macaulay, in his well-known passage on the position of the clergy at this time, tells us that if, after years of service in a nobleman's house, the chaplain was given a living, "with his cure he was expected to take a wife". The wife found for him had usually been in the patron's service, and in many cases had been the patron's mistress. "The relation between divines and hand-maidens", says Macaulay, "was a theme for endless jest."

These handmaidens, as Macaulay must have known, were often of as good family, and sometimes of better, than were the clergymen or schoolmasters whom they married. Among them there were women of independent character, who, in spite of the intolerable difficulties of their situation, had kept their self-respect, acquired knowledge, and gained the esteem of the family they served. Some among them even married well, in the sense that their husbands were men of character and industry; and they must have brought up families better prepared to take a place in the world of work and thought than they had been themselves. Among these women was Hannah Woolley (or, as she sometimes spelled it, Wolley).

Her name is well known to-day to collectors of books on cookery and the domestic arts. She was born in 1623, and was left an orphan and entirely dependent on her own exertions at the age of fourteen. She lived through the reign of Charles the First and the Commonwealth; and in 1674, when Charles the Second had reigned for fourteen years, she was alive, well, and thanking God for His many mercies to her. After this date we have no further record of her life.

There are in the British Museum five of her books, some of which went through several editions. The first, *The Ladies' Directory in choice experiments and curiosities of Preserving and Candying both Fruit and Flowers*, was published in 1661. This book, *The Cook's Guide* (1664), *The Ladies' Delight* (1672), and the first edition of *The Queen-like Closet* (1670), consists of receipts for preserving, cooking, physicking, and serving at table. *The Gentlewoman's Companion* (dated 1675) and the Supplement to the second (1675) and later editions of *The Queen-like Closet*, also contain general directions for behaviour in Society.

All Hannah Woolley's books are of interest in giving us more than a glimpse of the diet, the table-manners, and the social customs of people of quality in the time of the Protectorate and Restoration. For my purpose, however, the most important part of her writings is the autobiographical material contained in the Supplement to the second edition of *The Queen-like Closet* and in *The Gentlewoman's Companion*. From this material it is possible to reconstruct the life of Hannah Woolley from the age of fourteen to the age of fifty-one, and to gain a clear insight into the motives which impelled her to write. One was a frank desire to make money for herself and her family, and the other was a desire to help the portionless gentlewomen of her day to maintain themselves in independence. In *The Gentlewoman's Companion* she apologizes for troubling ladies "with any passages of my life". "A Person of Honour", she says, "engag'd me to do so if for no other reason than stop the mouths of such who may be so maliciously censorious as to believe I pretend to what I cannot perform. It is no ambitious design of gaining a name in print (a thing as rare for a Woman to endeavour, as obtain) that put me on this bold undertaking but"—and the more we know of her the more real does this motive appear—"the meer pity I have entertain'd for such Ladies, Gentlewomen and others, as have not received the benefits of the tyth of the ensuing accomplishments" (p. 15).[1]

She only mentions her own family twice, once to tell us (when she is recounting as part of her qualifica-

---

[1] My quotations from *The Gentlewoman's Companion* are from the edition of 1682 (a reprint in better type of the first edition dated 1675), and those from the Supplement to *The Queen-like Closet* from the first edition of 1674. I refer to *The Gentlewoman's Companion* as "G.C." and to *The Queen-like Closet* as "Q.C." Page references to *Q.C.* refer, unless otherwise stated, to the Supplement, which is separately paged from the rest of the book.

tions as a governess the many afflictions she has
undergone) that she lost her father and mother when
very young; and again when, in the Supplement to
The Queen-like Closet, she is giving directions to ladies
to be their "own Chirurgiens and Physicians, unless
the case be desperate", and she bids them "take notice
that my Mother and Elder Sisters were very well
skilled in Physick and Chirurgery, from whom I
learnt a little" (p. 8). It is clear, however, that she
had been better educated than the majority of girls
of her time, for it was by teaching and not by service
that she began to earn her living. "When I was
fourteen years old", she says, "I began to consider
how I might improve my time to the best advantage,
not knowing at that age anything but what reason
and fancy dictated to me. Before I was fifteen, I was
intrusted to keep a little School, and was the sole
Mistris thereof. This course of life I continued till
the age of Seventeen, when my extraordinary parts
appear'd more splendid in the eyes of a Noble Lady
in this Kingdom, than really they deserv'd; who
praising my Works with appellation of Curious Pieces
of Art, was infinitely pleased therewith. But understanding withal, that I understood indifferently the
smooth Italian, and could sing, dance and play on
several sorts of Musical Instruments, she took me from
my School, and greedily entertained me in her House
as Governess of her only Daughter" (*G.C.*, p. 17).

Hannah Woolley breaks into her narrative to give
a list of the accomplishments that she is now ready to

impart to other ladies. This seems to indicate that book-learning may have held a subordinate place in the time-table of her school. "Things I pretend greatest Skill in", are, she says:

"Works wrought with a Needle, all Transparent Works, Shell-work, Moss-work, also Cutting of Prints, and adorning Rooms or Cabinets, or stands with them.

"All kinds of Beugle-works upon wyers, or otherwise.

"All manner of Pretty Toys for Closets.

"Rocks made with Shell or in Sweets.

"Frames for Looking-glasses, Pictures or the Like.

"Feathers of Crewel for the corners of Beds.

"Preserving all kind of Sweet-meats wet and dry.

"Setting out of Banquets.

"Making Salves, Oyntments, Waters, Cordials, healing any wounds not desperately dangerous.

"Knowledge in discerning the Symptoms of most Diseases and giving such Remedies as are fit in such Cases.

"All manner of Cookery.

"Writing and Arithmetic.

"Washing black or white Sarsnets.

"Making Sweet Powders for the Hair, or to lay among Linnen.

"All these and several things beside too tedious here to relate, I shall be ready to impart to those who are desirous to learn" (G.C., pp. 15–17).

She had kept her school for only two years when she was called away by this appreciative lady, who died less than a year later. But in that short time Hannah Woolley had added considerably to the list of her accomplishments. Speaking of this lady she says: "Unto this honourable Person, I am indebted for the basis, or ground-work of my Preserving and Cookery, by my observation of what she ordered to be done. By this Ladies means I became acquainted with the Court, with a deportment suitable thereunto" (*G.C.*, p. 18).

We are not surprised that now, when at the staid age of eighteen Hannah was free, another lady of quality was anxious to entertain her. The new lady was, she says, "in no way inferiour to the former". In her house she lived for seven years. "At first I was governess to those of her Children whose forward virtue sufficiently declared the goodness of the Stock from whence they came" (*G.C.*, p. 18).

We do not know how long Hannah Woolley was governess to these children, but it was during her stay of seven years in this household that her career as a professional teacher of children ended, and that she attained the post of which she was so proud. "Time and my Lady's good opinion of me", she says, "constituted me afterwards her Woman, her Stewardess, and her Scribe or Secretary. By which means I appear'd as a person of no mean authority in the Family" (*G.C.*, p. 18). Hannah Woolley is always frank, and she expresses pleasure that by this change

"I profited in Externals"; but she does not forget the
things of the mind. Here, in the few years that
remained before her marriage, she had her first real
opportunity of satisfying her hunger for knowledge
of a world larger than a little school or a housekeeper's
room. "I treasured up", she says, "things necessary to
my understanding, having an happy opportunity so
to do, not only by hearing that ingenious and agreeable
discourse interfac'd between my Lady and Persons of
Honour, but also by inditing all her Letters; in the
framing and well fashioning of which (that I might
encrease my Ladies esteem) I took indefatigable
pains. There were not any who both wittily and
wisely had publisht their Epistles to the view of the
world whom I had not read, and on all occasions did
consult: those which I placed in my greatest esteem
were the Letters of Mr. Ford, Mr. Howard, Mr.
Loveday, and Monsieur Voiture" (*G.C.*, pp. 18–19).

Throughout her life, Hannah Woolley felt strongly
how much the art of letter-writing was neglected.
In the Supplement to *The Queen-like Closet* she writes:
"I do daily find that in Writing most Women are to
seek. They many times spend their time in Learning
a good Hand; and their English and Language is,
The one not easie to understand, The other weak and
impertinent. I meet with Letters my self sometimes,
that I could even tear them as I read them, they are
so full of impertinency and so tedious" (*Q.C.*, p. 104).

In this house Hannah's literary education went on
apace. She read daily to her lady poems, plays, and

romances. She learnt "where to place my accents, how to raise and fall my voice, where lay the emphasis of the expression" (*G.C.*, p. 19). Her lady took great delight in "romances of the best sort", such as those which Hannah Woolley advises young gentlewomen to read. "There are few Ladies mention'd therein", she says, "but are Character'd what they ought to be"; and the men have such "magnanimity, virtue, gallantry, patience, constancy and courage" as "might intitle them, worthy Husbands to the most deserving of the female sex" (*G.C.*, p. 14).

Her lady was also "very well verst in the propriety of the French Tongue, there was not anything published by the Virtuosi of France which carefully and chargeably she procured not; this put me upon the understanding of that Language, she was so well experienc'd therein, which is as great an Ornament for young Ladies, as the Learned Tongues of which the Academical Studioso boasts more than a common understanding" (*G.C.*, pp. 19–25).

Hannah Woolley has told us that at eighteen, or before, she had learnt the deportment suitable to a court, but now she says that she added, "Courtly Phrases and Graces, so how to express myself with the attendancy of a becoming air. And as I gather'd how to manage my Tongue gracefully and discreetly; so I thought it irrequisite to let my hands to lye idle, I exercised them daily in Carving at Table. And when any sad accident required their help in Physick and Chyrurgery, I was ready to be assisting; in those two excellent Arts in this place I acquired a competent knowledge" (*G.C.*, p. 20).

A mere glance at her own bills of fare for people of "quality", and even for people of "lesser quality", shows that carving in those days was no light task. How seriously she took her work in Physick and Chyrurgery, we learn from her own words. The lady, she says, "finding my genius, and being of a Charitable temper to do good amongst her poor Neighbours, I had her purse at command to buy what Ingredients might be required to make Balsoms, Salves, Oynt-ments, Waters for Wounds, Oyls, Cordials, and the like: besides she procured such knowledge for me from her Physicians and Chirurgiens (who were the best that all England could afford) and also bought many Books for me to read, that in short time, with the help of those Worthy men before mentioned, I soon became a Practitioner, and did begin with Cut fingers, Bruises, Aches, Agues, Head-ach . . . etc. . . . and any thing which is commonly incident; and in all those cures God was pleased to give me good success" (*Q.C.*, p. 8).

It is little wonder that others besides her lady were aware that there was in their midst a woman of unusual powers and accomplishments. Hannah Woolley gives us, with the frank sense of her own value that is one of her charms, her reason for quitting the post where she had done and learnt so much. "In short time", she says, "I became skilful, and stayed [i.e. staid] enough to order an House, and all offices belonging to it; and gained so great an esteem among the Nobility and Gentry of two Counties, that I was necessitated to yield to the importunity of one I dearly loved, that I might free myself from the tedious Caresses of a many more" (*G.C.*, p. 20).

She married, she tells us, at the age of twenty-four (i.e. in 1647). Her husband was Mr. Woolley (or Wolley), who had been master of a Free School at Newport Pond in Essex, fourteen years before, and who was still there. We know from her own words that her marriage was a happy one. But happy marriage did not mean for her a life of leisure. She tells us that during these years in Essex it was not only on her own family that she exercised her medical skill. Before she left the service of her lady she called herself a "practitioner". Now she tells us that she used her knowledge "among my neighbours, friends and acquaintances". She had four sons of her own to bring up. In addition to these, "We", she says, "having many Boarders my skill was often exercised amongst them". We have no reason to believe that the sanitary conditions of Hannah Woolley's house were worse than those of other boarding-houses of her day, and from what we know of her, it is probable that the diet and general care given to her boarders were far better than was usual. But she says of these boys, "oftentimes they got mishaps when they were playing, and oftentimes fell into distempers; as Agues, Feavors, Meazles, Small-pox, Consumption and many other Diseases". And she adds with pride that "unless

they were desperately ill their Parents trusted me
without the help of any Physician or Chirurgien"
(*Q.C.*, p. 12).

After some years of this active life in Essex the
Woolleys lived at "Hackney, near London", where
"we had above three score Boarders", and where, she
says, and we can well believe it, "I had many more
Trials for my Skill both at home and abroad" (*Q.C.*,
p. 15). Hannah Woolley had never lacked courage.
While she still "belonged to a Noble Lady" she tells
that a woman in labour near by, "had fallen into
strong convulsive fits", and that arriving with her
remedies she secured for her "a safe delivery". By
the time that she reaches Hackney her courage has
grown. She dare not tell, she says, the remedies she
used in really difficult cases. "Because there is in
those cases a good Judgment required, and I use those
things, in those cases which are not Common Receipts,
which may as well Kill, as Cure; . . . Experience,
with much Reading must give that understanding"
(*Q.C.*, "To the Reader"). Her remedies were perhaps
no better and no worse than those of an average
apothecary of her day; more or less harmless cordials
and possets are intermingled with forms of treatment
which were both disgusting and dangerous.

Mr. Woolley died, perhaps about 1660, and the
Registry of the Vicar General of the Archbishop of
Canterbury contains for April 16th, 1666, the record
of a marriage certificate for "Francis Challinor of
St. Margaret's Westminster, Gent, widower about 45,

and Hannah Woolley of the same, Widow, about 43, at St. Margaret's Westminster". Mr. Challinor (or Chaloner as she spells it) also died, and in the advertisement to the Supplement to *The Queen-like Closet* (1674 edition) she says that she is to be found "at Mr. Richard Woolley's House in the Old Bailey in Golden Cup Court. He is Master of Arts, and Reader at St. Martin's Ludgate". He may very probably have been her son. In his house she sold "several remedies for several Distempers, at reasonable Rates", and also kept a registry office and training-school for servants. "Likewise", she says, "if any Gentlewomen or other Maids who desire to go forth to Service, and do want Accomplishment for the same: For a reasonable Gratuity I shall inform them what I am able." She will, too, recommend them to her friends, if she finds that they are "Ingenious and deserving, or obliging in their disposition; neat and cleanly in their Habit; not too costly but decent, lively Spirited, not bold; and that can give me a good account of their parentage."

If her first husband died about 1660, she must have begun in her first widowhood to attempt to make a living for herself and her children among the often unscrupulous tradesmen who combined in the seventeenth and early eighteenth centuries the occupations of bookseller and publisher. Her first little books of receipts seem to have been successful, and after her second marriage she still used for publishing purposes the name of Hannah Woolley.

The publisher of *The Cook's Guide* (1661) and *The Ladies' Directory* (1662) was Mr. Peter Dring, who also sold her "sovereign pills" and cordials.

The confused state of the law of copyright in the seventeenth century seems a few years afterwards to have enabled a Mr. Dorman Newman to treat her as unscrupulous theatre-managers are now sometimes accused of treating dramatic authors. He arranged for her to write a combined cookery-book and treatise on social behaviour, kept the manuscript indefinitely by him, entrusted it in her absence to someone else to revise, and sent her the proofs to correct. When she protested, he denied liability and made a fresh bargain with her to correct the new version. She did so, and allowed the book to appear under her name. Finally he refused to pay what he had promised.

The book appeared as *The Gentlewoman's Companion* (dated 1675, but with a preface, signed Hannah Woolly, dated November 10, 1672). He had a worn copper-plate, representing a lady with curls and a necklace, which had originally stood for a Mrs. Gilley. He obliterated the name and used it as a frontispiece, with the implication that it was a portrait of Hannah Woolley. The book contains, even after her correction, a good deal of second-rate padding by some literary hack, including many conventional references to Latin mythology, and ends with twenty pages of dull "Pleasant discourses and Witty Dialogues", which are wholly unlike Hannah Woolley's own style.

She at once took her only remedy as the law then stood. She wrote a Supplement to her book of receipts, *The Queen-like Closet* (which had been first published by Richard Lowndes[1] in 1670), in which she vigorously repudiated the published version of *The Gentlewoman's Companion* (which she refers to by its second title as *The Ladies' Guide*), and challenges Mr. Newman to print her original manuscript. "He would do himself much right", she says, "to print the same verbatim" (*Q.C.*, p. 133).[2] Both books ran through several editions in the next ten years, but *The Queen-like Closet*, which reached a fifth edition, was the more successful.

In the Supplement to *The Queen-like Closet* she thanks God that she herself is in excellent health, and among the many instances that she gives of cures that she had effected, she tells us: "I cured my own Son of an Impostume in the Head, and of a deep Consumption, after the Physicians had given him over"; and again: "And for the palsie, whether Dead or Shaking, I am sure none can give better Remedies . . . there is none that hath been more afflicted with

[1] R. Lowndes of Duck Lane, near Smithfield, who also, like Mr. Peter Dring, sold her pills and powders. Dunton says that he was "a sincere honest dealer". (Plomer's *Dictionary of Printers*.)

[2] Clavel, in his *Catalogue of Books* printed 1666–95 (p. 102), records that Woolley's *Gentlewoman's Companion* was copyrighted by D. Newman. He must therefore have been the man behind Mr. "Edward Thomas" for whom *The Gentlewoman's Companion or a Guide to the Female Sex* was printed. Mr. Newman was Mr. Dorman Newman; Plomer, in his *Dictionary of Printers*, says that "he was one of the largest publishers of his day". One is glad to learn that he went bankrupt in 1694.

it than my self, and (I humbly thank God for it) there is no Person more freer from it than myself, nor from any other Disease, and that is very much, I being now in my Two and fiftieth year" (*Q.C.*, p. 16). And she had other blessings: "I thank God," she exclaims, "though I have passed through many more Afflictions and Troubles than thousands of my Sex, yet I never had an ill Husband, nor undutiful Children, but (on the contrary) I have been marryed to two Worthy, Eminent, and brave Persons; and I have four Sons, as good Children as ever Woman did bear. . . . I give thanks and glory to Almighty God, for what benefits I have received from time to time: and especially for those Blessings which I do at this present enjoy; The lives and welfare of my Dear Children, The happy choice which two of them have made in their Wives, and that I have lived to see two sweet Babes from their Loyns. Such like comfort as this I wish to all Christians" (*Q.C.*, p. 140).

We do not know when she died, but she may perhaps have been alive at the age of sixty-one, when the fifth edition of *The Queen-like Closet* appeared in 1684; and she was probably dead before 1711, when, if living, she would have been eighty-eight, and when an edition of *The Gentlewoman's Companion* was brought out under the name of *The Complete Gentlewoman*, and with further insertions that are unlike her genuine work.

Hannah Woolley made no claim that all her writings on the domestic arts were original. She tells us, in the

"Epistle Dedicatory" to *The Gentlewoman's Companion*, that she borrowed freely from others. Still, she says, "there are some things treated in this Book that I have not met with in any Language, but are the Product of my Thirty Years Observation and Experience". In all branches of domestic work she regarded herself as an artist. In speaking of embroidery she says: "I have seen such Ridiculous things done in Work, as is an abomination to any Artist to behold." And as an instance she mentions a piece of embroidery she had seen, where Abraham and Sarah were dressed as "now-a-days"; and even worse, she has seen them made to "resemble pictures in ballads". It is this conscience in all she did that convinces me that it would be a delightful occupation to test some of Hannah Woolley's cookery receipts, as she begs ladies to do before they censure them. Unfortunately the domestic arrangements of few people nowadays allow them to take a fat red pig and a sprig of rosemary and throw into a pot of Rhenish wine. And the ingredients she used for her cure for melancholy, and in her cordials for all occasions, are no longer obtainable without a great expenditure of time and money.

But in Hannah Woolley's two most important works, *The Queen-like Closet* and *The Gentlewoman's Companion*, there is a great deal more than a curious collection of carefully tested receipts. It is true that we might as well go to Mrs. Beeton for an account of the relations of England and Ireland in the nineteenth century or

of the Oxford Movement, as to Hannah Woolley
for ideas on the fundamental religious and political
questions that led to the exile and restoration of the
Stuarts. The only references to national events in
her books are such statements as that she had with
her own hands prepared a banquet for Charles the
First. What she does give us is a picture of the mind
and opinions of a gentlewoman of the Church of
England, living a hard, shrewd, practical life, in
those troubled times. She describes *The Gentlewoman's
Companion* in her preface as a "Universal Companion
and Guide to the Female Sex in all Relations, Com-
panies, Conditions, and states of Life, even from
Child-hood down to Old age; from the Lady at the
Court, to the Cook-maid in the Country". The mere
study of the Table of Contents of this book is enough
to make the brain of a modern woman spin. It
contains everything which she thought of value in
her own books and in all those she had read on
domestic arts, besides her opinions and those of other
people on such subjects as education, marriage, and
dress. To take at random some points on which a
young gentlewoman might find herself in difficulty:
Suppose, Hannah Woolley says, that you have "a dear
Female Friend" whom you suspect of any "youth-
ful excursions", especially levity, and whom you would
like to reduce to "a better understanding"; then you
turn to this book and you will find instructions for
writing her a letter that so "mildly lays open her
errors" in such an "insinuating manner" that it can-

not fail to be taken in good part (*G.C.*, p. 309). Again, you are taught "How elegantly to complain of injuries done" (*G.C.*, p. 315). To turn to another subject: if a young gentlewoman has "a wandering eye" she will find a section especially meant for her, headed, "Of the Government of the Eye" (*G.C.*, p. 55). If she is troubled in her choice of a husband, there is this sage counsel: "Whatever you do, be not induced to marry one you have either abhorrency or loathing to" (*G.C.*, p. 134).

Hannah Woolley, although she regrets the waste of time spent on fashionable dress, and warns her readers not to allow their apparel "to exceed the Arithmetic of her Revenues", had no desire to be too rigid. "I do not deny", she says, "there is a kind of priveledge in youth for wearing fashionable Clothes, jewels and Diamonds, which Nature (who doeth nothing in vain) hath provided" (*G.C.*, p. 85). A lady, she maintains, should not altogether oppose "the torrent of the fashion then in being". "Should you now", she writes, "wear a Farthingal or a narrow brim'd Hat with a long crown, and a strutting Ruff (It is not long since such things were in fashion), a Jack-pudding could not attract more Boys after him, than would follow you" (*G.C.*, p. 90). At the same time she could write courageously against painting and patching, and the more serious evil of tight-lacing. She condemns those mothers and nurses who, "by cloistering you up in a Steel or Whale-bone prison, open a door to Consumption with many other dangerous inconveniences, as Crookedness: for Mothers striving to have their daughters small in the middle, do pluck and draw their bones awry" (*G.C.*, p. 120). On the other hand, speaking to the ladies of England, she says: "I would not have them by inconsiderate looseness run into a deformed corpulency, like the Venetian Ladies who seldom lace them selves at all" (*G.C.*, p. 121).

Her considered opinion is that ladies should approach "somewhat to the Mode of the Court (which is the source and foundation of fashions)" (*G.C.*, p. 90). If they live in a remote country place, from which they cannot themselves "resort to Court", then they should seek the acquaintance of "some prudent person who is frequently there, and by her pattern and direction order your habit with reference, as near as may be, to your quality, age and estate". Their own ingenuity, she tells them, will enable them to keep a great part of the fashion while reducing it "to suit your convenience, modesty and Christian deportment" (*G.C.*, p. 91). The summing up of her wisdom on dress is the same as that on other subjects. "Thus you see in all things (except Piety) Mediocrity, or the Golden-mean is to be observed" (*G.C.*, p. 121).

In *The Queen-like Closet* and *The Gentlewoman's Companion*, she is writing primarily for people of quality. To them she owed all the opportunities of her life; but while she is frankly anxious to please them, she is saved from servility by the fact that their views and hers were usually in perfect agreement. She takes for granted that in the social intercourse of the minor gentlefolk with the great people of quality a special set of manners is called for. "To persons of Quality in a higher rank than your own," she says, "be very attentive to what they say, lest you put them to the trouble of speaking things twice. Interrupt them not while they are speaking, but patiently expect till they have done." And again: "It is very unhandsome, when you contradict a Person of Quality, to answer him with, It is not so; if you are necessitated thereunto, do it by circumlocutions, I beg your Honours pardon: Madam, I beseech your Ladyship to excuse my presumption, if I say you mistake, etc." And once more: "If your love and respect to a Ladys Person, obligeth you to reprove a fault in her, do not say, Madam, you acted the part of a mad woman, in doing such a thing, but, had such a thing been left undone, you had neither disobliged your self or friend" (G.C., pp. 76–77). If a young lady is in the happy position, in a great house, of having charge of the sweet-meats, she must not send in refreshments to visitors in the afternoon regardless of their quality. If you have found out that they are "no greater, or so great as the Person who entertains them, then you may present one or two Dishes of Cream only, and a whipt Sillibub or other with about four Dishes of Sweet-meats . . . with Fruit and some kind of Wine of your own making" (Q.C., Part II, p. 342). What delightful refreshments were handed to persons of higher rank than the host and hostess is left to our imaginations.

Still, Hannah Woolley had been poor herself, and she had seen so much of the scandalous waste in great houses that her exhortations are not addressed only to the poor. It is women generally of whom she is speaking, when she says: "They are Fools who cannot tell what to do with scraps of meat" (Q.C., p. 99).

In writing of Love and Courtship, and admitting her debt "to the most able Professors and Teachers both here and beyond the Seas", she explains that she "durst not be so airy and light in my Treatise about Ladies Love and Courtship as some of the French Authors have been, but I have taken out of them what I found most taking with our English Gentry" (G.C., Epistle Dedicatory). In religious matters, except for admonition to daily prayers, the most important advice she gives is to "get that Catechism the Government has made choice of for you, by heart; by the practice of which you will be enabled to perform your duty to God and man" (G.C., p. 31).

Of parental authority she is an ardent advocate. Difficulties between parents and children constantly arose in those days. It was frequent, she says, "for youth not only to deride the imperfections of their Parents, but forge and pretend more than they have" (G.C., p. 33). Parents were undoubtedly severe, for she feels it necessary to advise young gentlewomen whose ages range from six to sixteen that they should not "for any temporal benefit, or to be free from the severity of their Parents, wish their death" (*G.C.*, p. 34). Growing up, even, did not mend matters. "Think not," she says, "though grown up to Woman's estate, that you are freed from Obedience." It was not enough for these poor children to conform outwardly, they must analyse their motives. "Let not your motive thereunto be that of worldly prudence fearing to displease Your Parents, lest they should diminish your intended Portion, and so be a loser thereby" (*G.C.*, p. 35). And then: "But of all the acts of disobedience that of marrying against the consent of Parents is the highest. Children are so much the Goods and Chattles of a Parent, that they cannot without a kind of theft give themselves away without the allowance of those that have the right in them" (*G.C.*, p. 36). Let us hope her dutiful pupils did not find this advice in conflict with her other advice—that they should in no case marry where they had a positive aversion.

As Hannah Woolley describes it, marriage is not only a state of many and exacting duties, but one of complete subjection for women. Speaking to young girls, she says that she wishes "all such as are entred into the Honourable State of Matrimony, to be loyal and loving Subjects". Indulgence on the part of the wife to her husband's wanderings is inculcated: "If you marry one very young, bear with his youth. . . . Youth will have his swing: time will reclaim, and discretion will bring him home at last" (*G.C.*, p. 135).

Though she says much more on this subject, it is so entirely the expression of the well-known opinions of her time that there is little worth quoting. But her reasons for looking after a husband's comfort appeal to the common sense of the women of all periods. "Let him not wait for his meals, lest by so staying his affairs be disorder'd or impeded. And let what you provide be so neatly and cleanly drest, that his fare, though ordinary, may engage his appetite, and disengage his fancy from Taverns, which many are compell'd to make use of by reason of the continual and daily dissatisfactions they find at home" (*G.C.*, pp. 160–161). There is, however, one passage on marriage, in this curious book, where I think that she is speaking of her personal experience. "If", she says, "the choice on both sides be good and well ordered; there is nothing in the World that is more beautiful, more comfortable. It is a sweet society, full of trust and loyalty. It is a fellowship not of hot distempered love, but endeared affection" (*G.C.*, p. 156).

One turns with relief to a subject on which she undoubtedly speaks throughout from her own experience: that of education. She treats of the education of children of both sexes and of that of girls and women in particular. Writing before Locke or Fénelon, she makes a protest against the extreme severity of the governesses she has known, and begs all parents to exercise care in their choice. "They who undertake the difficult Employ of being an Instructress or Governess of Children, should be persons of no mean

birth and breeding, civil in deportment, of an extraordinary winning and pleasing conversation. They
should not be rash in expression, nor severe in correcting such as are under their charge; but instruct
them with all mildness, cheerfully incouraging them
in what they are injoyned to perform, not suddenly
striking, nor startling them with a loud rebuke, which
causes in some an aversness to what they should love,
imbittering all the former delight they had in learning."
"Blows", she goes on to say, "are fitter for beasts than
rational creatures." Then Hannah Woolley gives an
example of what she mildly calls "unadvised severity".
A governess in Dorsetshire, she tells us, "being somewhat aged and suspecting her strength was not able
to grapple with active youth, called up her Maid to
her assistance, with whose help she so cruelly chastised
a young Gentlewoman for some fault she had committed, that with grief and shame she died a little
time after". She states that this is only one of the cases
for which she can vouch. "But", she says, "I forbear
to publish the shame of such inconsiderate rashness."
It is not only to governesses but to mothers that she
has to say a word on this subject. "Some Mothers"
there are, "whose presence makes their children
tremble." Such mothers "frighten their love into an
abhorrency of their sight" (G.C., pp. 5–7).

But it would be a mistake to think that Hannah
Woolley's idea of mildness was the same as ours to-day,
or that she advised ruining the characters of children
by over-indulgence. Again, it is the "golden mean"

that she advocates. "Be", she says in the same section, "the incessant tormentor of her Sloth, lest by becoming burdensome to others she at length become so to herself; by which means her understanding starves, and her body contracts an Hospital of Diseases. This you may remedy by suffering her not to sleep over-long, lest the spirits be over-dull'd" (*G.C.*, p. 10). It is in this connection that we have the only hint that she gives, although she tells us that she was disabled from employment by much sickness, that she had felt the strain of her incessant overwork from girlhood. It is, too, a passage that gives insight into her character; it shows her capable, for the benefit of others, of pointing out that she had had in youth a real and unlovable failing. She begs parents not to choose governesses who are very young for their children. "For they", she says, "will have sufficient to do to govern themselves." "What I now declare", she goes on, "is the fruit of experience, having had too great a charge in this matter, when I was very young, and do know how defective I was then in my duty, since I became a Mother of Children, having now more tenderness to youth; and can speak it knowingly, that a mild moderate way is to be preferred before rigor and harshness and that correction of words is better than that of blows" (*G.C.*, p. 40). This tenderness and her faith in the moderate way grew with the growth of her children. Speaking, when she was fifty-one years old, to parents of the need of teaching their children "the Principles of True

Religion" and to encourage them to keep duly to "Church and to Family Duties", she says: "Let them be lovingly and quietly Governed: not with perpetual Chiding and Brawling, but treat with them mildly and gently; unless you find them Refractory to your Commands; if so, then some Austere language must be used." And, "if by ill-Fate (after all this care) you should have a rebellious and refractory Child, your frequent Prayers to Almighty God will be the only way to reclaim them" (*Q.C.*, pp. 141–143). There is here no mention of corporal punishment; "some austere words and frequent prayers" have become for Hannah Woolley the last resort.

It was not only in protesting against cruelty and violence in the treatment of children that Hannah Woolley did service to the education of her time. From first to last she advises a careful study of the child's mind, an understanding of the limits of its powers, and an adaptation of the method to the individual. Even nursery-maids should be those who naturally love children. She admonishes them, "be not churlish or dogged to them, but merry and pleasant and contrive and invent pretty pastimes agreeable for their age" (*G.C.*, p. 293). For this work a girl should not be "sluggish nor heavy-headed". Both parents and governesses in their teaching of children should have a special regard to "what their genious is inclined to: for that to be sure they will be excellent at. Let them be fully employed, but with diversity of things; that will be a delight to them" (*Q.C.*, p. 142).

But the subject on which Hannah Woolley had thought most, and about which she was most troubled, was the education of girls; and again she is in advance of the current ideas of her time. It is true that there is nothing in her writings that would make us suppose that her curriculum for them would have been anything but a curious hotchpotch of mosswork and mathematics, of ancient languages and cordials, modern languages and powders to whiten the skin. Still her own thoroughness and industry must have been infectious, and she had the true faith in learning. She says of it that "it not only fortifies the best inclinations, but enlargeth a mean capacity to a great perfection". She draws a pathetic picture of ladies from the country who have "no agreeable discourse", as those have who are well read; they stand, she says, "like so many Mutes or Statues when they have happened into the company of the ingenious; their quaint expressions have seem'd to them Arabian Sentences; and have stared like so many distracted persons, in that they could hear the sound of English, and yet understand but here and there a word of their own Language" (*G.C.*, p. 11).

The very first words of her Introduction to *The Gentlewoman's Companion* are, "The right Education of the Female Sex, as it is in a manner every where neglected, so it ought to be generally lamented. Most in this depraved later Age think a Woman learned and wise enough if she can distinguish her Husbands bed from another's" (*G.C.*, p. 1). She complains that men think the use of women on the earth was merely for propagation "and to keep its humane Inhabitants sweet and clean; but by their leaves, had we the same Literature, he would find our brains as fruitful as our bodies" (*G.C.*, p. 2). And again: "I cannot but complain of, and must condemn the great negligence of Parents, in letting the fertile ground of their Daughters lie fallow, yet send the barren Noddles of their sons to the University, where they stay for no other purpose than to fill their empty Sconces with idle Notions to make a noise in the Countrey" (*G.C.*, p. 2). She complains again and again of this neglect of parents, and begs mothers to teach their own children, and to teach "with their letters good manners". Girls are never absent from her mind. She cannot enough bewail "the careless neglect of Parents, who think neither God or Nature doth tie them to further regard of their Children than to afford them food, and make them strut in the fashion, learn them to dance and sing, and lastly lay up a considerable sum, for some person whom they value by his greatness not his goodness". This treatment of girls leads not only, she says, "to a daily breach of God's holy laws, but the Laws of Civil Society" (*G.C.*, p. 23).

The only practical means of improvement that Hannah Woolley suggests are reform in the home, and the more serious education of girls through greater care being taken in the choice of governesses. She had no dream of a college for women, as Mary Astell had twenty years later, although she may have lived to welcome that suggestion. How far such a scheme was from her hopes is shown pathetically by an extract from a model letter from a young gentlewoman of quality to her brother at Oxford. The young gentlewoman would like more frequent letters from her brother, "but", she writes, "I fear that your Studies will not admit you so much idle time as to think of me long, your Genius being wholly employed to hear the Sage Philosophers and the Muses, which I do imagine cannot choose but be very delightful" (*Q.C.*, p. 178).

Mary Astell was a woman of means, and although her trained understanding and social sympathies made the condition of all women of her time of importance to her, her main preoccupation and her best writing are given to the pathetic waste of opportunity in loveless marriage and idle spinsterhood. Hannah Woolley had been left by her parents' death with no means of livelihood except from her own earnings, and the fate of other girls in that position is always in her mind. Many young women, she tells us, were left penniless because their parents had been "undone". Sometimes it happens that friends and trustees are "neglectful of those in their Charge, have spent all that which was left them, and then exposed them to the mercy of the World without Education or Money". "Truly," she says, "I have taken this pains to impart these things for the general good of my Country, as well as my own, and have done it with the more willingness since I find so

many Gentlewomen forced to serve, whose Parents
and Friends have been impoverished by the late
Calamities, viz., the late Wars, Plague, and Fire,
and to see what mean places they are forced to be in,
because they want Accomplishments for better" (*Q.C.*,
Part II, p. 340). In such cases, "The poor Mother, she
employs her self in some what or other to maintain
her self, and the younger Children, who are not yet
able to take care of themselves: and for the Elder
ones they are forced to Service" (*Q.C.*, p. 137).
Hannah Woolley never thinks of them as having
knowledge enough to become teachers. Her object is
not to help them to escape from service, but to prepare
them for it, to encourage them to exert themselves,
to learn everything possible, that they may become
fit to hold posts in great houses such as she had
held, and not the posts which she describes as "but
slavish" (*Q.C.*, p. 137). She constantly warns young
women "who though well-born are notwithstanding
by indigency necessitated to serve some Persons of
Quality" that they must forget the past. "I would
not have you", she tells them, "look upon your condition as to what it hath been, but what it is" (*G.C.*,
p. 285). "If your Father hath had large Revenues,
and could talk loudly of his Birth, and so [you] may
think this servile life beneath you, yet thank God you
can do something for an honest livelihood, and be
never the less submissive; for if you are a Servant,
you must do what becomes a Servant" (*G.C.*, p. 288).
But although many young gentlewomen in this

position were forced to content themselves by being chambermaids, Hannah Woolley holds out a hope that they may secure better posts. The reason of their lowly position, she repeats, is that they have not the accomplishments of a "Waiting-woman or House-keeper". Such accomplishments "incline Ladies to covet their company, sit at Table and have a command in the House, respect from the rest of the Servants, wear good clothes, and have a considerable sallary; instead thereof the meanness of their qualifications render them only fit companions for Grooms and Foot-boys" (*G.C.*, p. 286). "Learn", she says, "whatever you can, and slight no opportunity which may advance your knowledge to the height of your birth" (*G.C.*, p. 284). She tells girls later: "observe every one how they do order their Houses, and how they do make this or that; and what you cannot remember, that write down, that it may stead you another time". She tells us of the girls who came to her in Golden Cup Court for instruction, when she started her training-school, that some of them were "very well accomplisht (those I find to be the most humble and willing to please). Another sort there be which have little in them; yet none but great Places will serve them; which when they have wearied themselves to find, and at last miss of what they have propounded to themselves, they are ready to run any extravagant Course still to purchase fine Cloaths, than to conform to any Civility or Manners, or to take the Advice of those who would assist them.

Some who have apt Wits and that Dame Nature hath been favourable to, they are courted to be Players: Some other of them to Bawdy-Houses. Some are tempted to steal. . . ." (Q.C., p. 134). She can remember cases where young gentlewomen, by no fault of their own, have sunk to a condition so squalid that they cannot even hope to enter service in any respectable house. "It hapneth oft-times", she says, "that a Gentleman having a good Estate but many Children, he and the care of a good Mother together doth make a very good shift to bring them all up (in appearance to the eye of the World) very handsomly: their attire being such as becomes his or her Children; their Education such as is fitting for, or the best which can be obtained in that place they live in; this they do till some of the Eldest are Women grown, and by that time they are considering how to bestow them in the World, finding the Charge to be too great for them." "If", she goes on to say, "an Elder one Marry; although there be one less in the Family, yet [she] carries more with her; than, if she had stayed would have been spent upon her." Even if the parents face this loss, "Her Husband perhaps in a short time, by playing the ill fellow is quite ruined, and his Wife turned home to her Parents again, with a Child or two to provide for. Where after a while, she cannot abide to hear her Husband blamed, neither is she willing to burden her Parents so much: she endeavours to get into some good Service, to be Nurse, and leaves her Child or Children with them."

Here Hannah breaks into her tale to say, truly, "She hath her affliction and doth waste herself with grief and sorrow". But the parents and the other members of the family suffer, too. "The parents find themselves so burdened that they must needs send some of the rest out to Service; and here they come to London, perhaps to some Cozin or Friend, thinking to get some place or other quickly, but find it a hard business. Their Friends beginning to grumble at their being; their Cloaths beginning to wear out, and all their mony spent; then do they find themselves in a desperate Condition, and do seek some place or other to Lodge in, and are content to be imployed in any honest way to get a penny, till they procure a Service; being not willing to return to their parents to add to their grief" (*Q.C.*, pp. 135-137).

Writing before any system of life insurance, or even of safe investment for savings, Hannah Woolley implores parents to remember that at any moment their daughters might find themselves in such a desperate condition, and to prepare them to meet it with courage and prudence. "Let them not", she says, "have command of your Purse, neither let them be without a little; and as they manage that give them more." "Teach them to be Housewifely in their Cloathes, and sparing of them. Let them learn the way of Housekeeping by acting your Commands. Let them know how to entertain Friends and to be Courteous to Strangers and loving to your Servants, not domineering over them." She begs all parents, "(be their Estates never so good and their Revenues large) to endeavour the gentile education of their Daughters, encouraging them to learn whatever opportunity offers, worthy a good estimation". "Now," she says, "if there be a treasury laid up within by education (by which they may live without an Estate their parents shall leave them) in some honest and creditable employment, their position will be so established that nothing almost but sickness or death can make an alteration therein."

We may smile at the intense seriousness with which Hannah Woolley gives young gentlewomen instructions "to dress up a chimney very fine for the summer time, as I have often done", or to "make pigge eat like lamb", or to "dye stockings black". But to know such arts might be the only means of escape from the life of the scullery or the degradation of the slums of old London; and, as Hannah Woolley knew from her own life, the acquirement of them might have a touch of heroism in it.

She thinks of those girls who have followed her advice, those who "keep close to their business (not shewing themselves in the Streets but when they have just occasion to go forth). These last", she declares, "shall never lack my assistance." And practical woman as Hannah Woolley was, memories of her own girlhood make her exclaim, "I do love such with my heart" (Q.C., p. 134).

A PHILOSOPHER AND HIS DAUGHTER

CHAPTER II

A PHILOSOPHER AND HIS DAUGHTER

IT is a disquieting reflection that those who come after us will judge, in great measure, of the tone and temper of our time by the books which are now most popular.

Lord Halifax's *Advice to a Daughter*, written about 1688, not only enjoyed great popularity in its day, but held its ground for a century. We know, from their own testimony, the admiration in which it was held by people as intellectually sensitive as Steele, Addison, and Lady Mary Wortley Montagu. It is therefore no surprise to find that the essay has literary force, charm of style, and good sense. Another cause of the great attraction of the book lay for its first readers, and lies for us, in the fact that Lord Halifax, a thinker of real importance, was actuated in making this New Year's gift to a little girl whose understanding was still "not very tall", by an affection rare even between father and daughter; an affection which still has power to move us, after more than two hundred years. Under the restraint of his language we feel that he cared passionately that Elizabeth should learn so to trim her boat as to make the best headway in the sea of life, with only such effort and suffering as he felt to be inevitable.

The book appeared at a moment when thoughtful

men were already troubled, not only by the lack of education among women of quality, but by their social and legal position. Men of decent feeling were also acutely conscious of the coarseness and utter levity with which any question that concerned women was treated.

Lord Halifax, at any rate, treated a woman seriously, and that woman was his own daughter. He tried to do, and succeeded in doing, one of the most difficult of all things. He put into readable and forcible language the result of his own experience of life, and his advice was valued; for we know that Elizabeth kept his New Year's gift on her table to the end of her life. It is not only Lord Halifax's beautiful and fresh common sense in practical matters, and his deep tolerance on religious questions, that sent the booklet through many editions. To many people his genuine interest in the minds and thoughts of little children, and his advice as to their treatment, must have come as a revelation of the way in which good feeling could be encouraged in the most intimate concerns of home-life. For there is such wisdom and penetration in what Lord Halifax says on the relations of mother and child, and even on those of mistress and servant, that the book should be read to-day, not simply from our interest in the past, but for the good of our living souls.

But the strange thing about this book is that on the subject of marriage, on which his fears and his desire to help are obviously greatest, Lord Halifax had nothing to say which is enlightened, and much which is simply poisonous.

Reading and re-reading this little book, I was fascinated by what he says on other subjects, and shocked and bewildered by what he says on this. To Lord Halifax, as to many people to-day, there were two separate regions of human life. First there was a region where a man or woman might hope by taking thought to leave the world better than he or she found it. Here humanity gave the motive-power which reason guided and controlled. But there was another region in which the laws of his loved country, sanctioned by his religion, must not be questioned. "Do not vainly imagine that things will be altered for your sake", he says, in speaking of what looks like injustice in the position of women in marriage. And in all that he says on this subject it seems as if a different man were writing. The tolerant and enlightened scholar, the humorous and patient observer, has no more to offer, in effect, than any mindless man of fashion. We only know that it is no common mind to which we are listening by a certain note of desperate sincerity. Where marriage is concerned, fear of the world and of slanderous tongues is uppermost in his thoughts, and he can offer Elizabeth no better advice than to "submit", and, having submitted, to observe carefully certain rules by which a humiliating position can best be made to serve her own personal advantage.

No student of the late seventeenth and early eighteenth centuries will call his fears groundless. "You are

at present", he says in his introductory letter, "the chief
Object of my Care, as well as of my kindness; which
sometimes throweth me into visions of your being
happy in the World, that are better suited to my
partial Wishes, than to my reasonable Hopes for you.
At other times, when my Fears prevail, I shrink as if
I was struck, at the Prospect of Danger to which a
young Woman must be exposed." Even his evident
pleasure in what he would have called "her parts"
makes him uneasy. She is "lively", and so more
liable to be hurt. "Such an early sprouting Wit", he
says, and warns her that he would have her wit
pruned "by so kind a Hand as that of a Father",
because: "Whilst you are playing full of Innocence,
the spiteful World will bite, unless you are guarded
by your caution."

The book itself Lord Halifax divides into the follow-
ing headings: Religion, Husband, House, Family and
Children, Behaviour, Friendships, Censure, Vanity,
Pride, and Diversions.

When he treats of Religion, Lord Halifax shows a
paternal anxiety that his daughter's hopes for the next
world shall in no way hinder her from making a
"good figure" in this. At the same time, there is little
or nothing in his advice under this heading inconsistent with his beautiful if limited definition of
Religion as "exalted Reason". As we should expect
from this definition, Lord Halifax is at his best in
speaking against superstition and recommending
tolerance and charity. "Religion", he says, "doth not

consist in believing the Legend of the Nursery, where Children with their Milk are fed with the Tales of Witches, Hobgoblins, Prophecies, Miracles." All this, he tells her, is so far from being religion that it is not sense. These mistakes are to be left off with her "hanging sleeves".

This extract throws light incidentally on the type of nurse to whom people of quality entrusted their children. Lady Mary Wortley Montagu, about sixty years later, speaking of her own governess, says: "It was none of her fault I am not this day frighted of witches and hobgoblins, or turned methodist." Lord Halifax's daughter and Lady Mary Wortley Montagu, if they could not throw off all the harm of such nurseries with their "hanging sleeves", certainly did not scandalize their circles by turning methodist.

Lord Halifax advises his daughter to keep to the religion in which she has been brought up, or rather, as he puts it, "that is grown up with you, both as it is the best in itself, and that the reason of staying in it upon that ground is somewhat stronger for your sex than it will perhaps be allowed to be for ours in respect that the voluminous enquiries into the truth by reading are less expected from you". But though she is to take the foundation of her faith at second-hand, she is told that the pleasures of religion are so great that "a wise epicure" would choose them. After that Lord Halifax writes of tolerance with feeling and conviction, in a passage so forcible it might with advantage be more often quoted. "Take heed", he

says, "of running into that common error of applying
God's judgments upon particular occasions. Our
weights and measures are not competent to make the
distribution either of His mercy or His justice."

Under the heading of "House, Family, and Children", he tells her that from her children she is not to
expect "a return of kindness", and then adds a sentence which might help any mother to understand
why that is an unreasonable expectation. The cause
of this is "not so much a defect in their good nature as
a shortness of thought in them". " . . . To be dis-
pleased for their own Good is a Maxim they are slow
to understand. So that you may conclude that the
first thoughts of your children will have no small
mixture of mutiny; which being so natural, you must
not be angry, except you would increase it. You must
deny them as seldom as you can, and when there is no
avoiding it, you must do it gently." And finally, "in
your treatment your Indulgence is to have the broader
Mixture, that Love rather than Fear, may be the
Root of their Obedience".

On the subject of servants, Lord Halifax's advice
might have led a thoughtful woman farther than he
intended. "The Inequality which is between you,
must not make you forget that Nature maketh no
such Distinction." And he speaks of "Returns of
Kindness" and "Good Usage" being as much due to
them as to "us".

Again, under the heading of "Expense" we have
this practical piece of wisdom. She must not, he tells

her, "give just Cause to the least Servant you have to complain of the want of what is necessary". In lesser matters in her own house good breeding is to be her guide; even her love for her children, he warns her, is not to make her forget good breeding. But he shows that he is still on firm ground; "take heed", he adds, of carrying "your good Breeding to such a height, as to be good for nothing and to be proud of it". Then he draws a picture of a lady who had apparently done this; a picture that is worthy of Addison or Steele at their best. She is, he says, "an empty airy Thing who sails up and down the House to no kind of purpose, and looks as if she came only to make a Visit". He speaks of her as "Her Emptiness", and tells how, after a useless day, thoroughly satisfied and "wrapped up in Flattery and fine Linen", she goes to bed. The husband of such a wife finds naturally "nor Order nor Quiet" in his house. Poor man, it is not much comfort to him that "the mistaken Lady" thinks to make amends for all this by having "a well-chosen petticoat". We can imagine the delight that such writing would give to Steele, who in his turn did so much to raise respect for those women who brought economy, order, and kindness into home life.

The art of laying out money wisely is, he tells Elizabeth, "not attained to without a great deal of Thought". And this, he points out, is especially true of a wife, because she is accountable to her husband for her mistakes in it. In one of his daughter's quality, Lord Halifax extremely dislikes "an undecent Thrift".

In clothes she must avoid "too much Gaudy", and she is not to value herself on "an embroidered Gown", nor to look for respect from what he calls "fine Trappings". "A full Attendance and well chosen Ornaments for your House will", he adds, "make you a better Figure, than too much glittering in what you wear." Under the heading of "Expense" he gives a maxim applicable to situations even more difficult than that of a seventeenth-century lady of quality, accountable to her husband for her part in the expenditure of what is grandly called "his Revenues". "Try everything first in your Judgment, before you allow it a place in your Desire."

After this admirable advice on home life, Lord Halifax says with obvious regret, "It is time now to lead you out of your House into the World". In his own political life he had felt the necessity for caution, for he says in his *Miscellanies*: "There is so much Danger in talking that a Man strictly wise can hardly be called a sociable Creature." The enemy, he warns her, "is abroad". She must "shorten her line of liberty". If she should allow herself to go to the utmost of what is lawful, those who are "at watch" will "begin to count on her". Elizabeth has to learn that in this society, "Behaviour towards men" is such a "nice affair" that she must keep careful watch on her eyes. "Civility may be taken as Invitation." He tells her that it is not enough to keep from "Criminal Engagements", she must even avoid all conduct that "raiseth a Discourse". Elizabeth was, we know, very young; but she is not too young to have impressed on her that she must make "a good Figure" as she grows old. "Every seven years" he advises her to make some alteration in dress, "towards the Graver Side, and not be like the Girls of Fifty who resolve to be always young". He speaks of "old Butterflies", who must needs go to Bartholomew Fair to look after the young folk or "who pretendeth to be pulled to a Play". Of course, he points out scornfully, they really enjoy these things themselves and use the young as an excuse. Poor old butterflies!

In the matter of Friendship—by which he means friendship among women—Lord Halifax's eyes are on "The Town." A violent friendship, if broken, ends in "a bag of Secrets" being untied; "they fly about like Birds let loose from a Cage and become the Entertainment of the Town". If your friend is not virtuous "the Town" will look upon you as her well-wisher, if not "her Partner in her Faults". When the slanderous tongues of which he was afraid speak ill of your friend —and this is the only kind word that he says in this section—you may be slow to believe them; but when what they have said is proved, you must beat "a fair and quick Retreat". And he goes on to argue that if you are too patient or show sympathy "the Company" may suspect that you would not be so zealous "if there was not a Possibility that that Case might be your own".

Under "Censure" we have the same care for what the "Town" will think. You must not proclaim "War to the World". You must "suppress your Impatience for Fools", because there are so many of them that it is unwise to provoke them.

In his few words on Pride we get, for a moment, away from the opinions of the "Town" to those of Lord Halifax the philosopher. A woman, he tells her again, is "not to be proud of her fine Gown, and when she hath less Wit than her Neighbours, to comfort herself that she hath more Lace". Some make quality an idol, and here Lord Halifax speaks with the warmth of conviction. "This Mistake is not", he says, "only senseless, but Criminal too, in putting a greater Price upon that which is a Piece of Good Luck, than upon Things that are valuable in themselves."

Under "Diversions" Lord Halifax does not forget that Elizabeth is young, and that in her married life she will need pleasure; although he hopes that she will not be like those ladies "who are engaged in a Circle of Idleness, where they turn round the whole Year, without the Interruption of a serious Hour". The real end of diversions is to "unbend our Thoughts when they are too much stretched by our Cares". He will approve if Elizabeth plays sometimes at cards, to "entertain Company" or "to divert herself". But, he goes on, "to deep Play there are great objections". The "Town" is in his mind again. It will ask spiteful questions. If she pays exactly, it will inquire where she got the money; and if she should owe to a man, he suggests to his little girl that she may have to pay by the loss of her virtue. This part of the book is cynical

GEORGE SAVILE, MARQUIS OF HALIFAX

(From the engraving by G. Haubouker, 1740)

enough, though there are still gleams of wit and good sense to be found in it.

But when he comes to consider marriage under the bare heading of "Husband", it is as though a prison door had been shut on the child, and her kind and wise father had become the warder, holding the keys against the intrusion of sincere thought or generous impulse. As to the choice of a husband, he tells her that which in her day she could hardly have lived to the advanced age of fifteen without knowing, that: "It is one of the Disadvantages belonging to your Sex, that young Women are seldom permitted to make their own Choice; their Friends' Care and Experience are thought safer Guides to them than their own Fancies; and their Modesty often forbiddeth them to refuse when their Parents recommend, though their inward Consent may not exactly go along with it." In this case he impresses on her that there is nothing to be done, but to endeavour "to make that easy that falleth to their Lot, and by a wise Use of every Thing they may dislike in a Husband, turn that by degrees to be very supportable, which, if neglected, might in time beget an Aversion". "You must first lay it down for a Foundation in general", he goes on, "that there is Inequality in the Sexes, and that for the better Economy of the World, the Men, who were to be the Lawgivers, had the larger Share of Reason bestowed upon them." Seeing that these may be hard sayings to his child, he hurries to give her consolation, but he has nothing

E

to offer but the time-worn resource of her beauty and her tears.

We feel that it is not a pleasant task that Lord Halifax has undertaken, and that at each revelation of the nature of the world, he knows what protest Elizabeth's understanding and her "sprouting Wit" would raise against injustice. "It is true", he admits, forestalling her natural indignation, "that the laws of Marriage run in a harsher Stile towards your Sex: Obey is an ungenteel Word . . . and so very unsuitable to the Excess of Good Manners which generally goes before it." He not only sees the difficulties, but he goes so far as to say: "It appeareth reasonable, that there might be an Exemption for extraordinary Women from Ordinary Rules." He even considers whether "those raised by Nature above the Level of their Sex" might not obtain "a Mitigation in their Particular of a Sentence that was given generally against Womankind". Against this he has nothing to advance except the fact that "causes of Separation are so very coarse" that the same modesty that prevented her from making her own choice will prevent her from obtaining her liberty. And, after all, Lord Halifax says: "For Disparity of Mind, which above all other Things requireth a Remedy, the Laws have made no Provision; so little refined are Numbers of Men by whom they are compiled." So, gaining confidence, he tells her as a fact, for which he offers no proof, that: "the supposition of your being the weaker Sex having without doubt a good Foundation, maketh it reasonable to subject it to the Masculine Dominion"; and argues that to right a few injustices "it is unwise to break into an Establishment upon which the Order of Human Society doth so much depend".

So, having instilled into Elizabeth that the male sex has given "a Sentence against Womanhood", that as a woman her reasoning powers are inferior, and that in cases of obvious injustice there is no remedy, Lord Halifax leaves the general subject to go into the particular question of how best to live with any one of the different types of husband which her "friends' Care and Experience" may provide for her. He seems to shrink from giving a definite name to the first kind of husband: a man who is from the beginning persistently faithless to his wife. He tells his child: "You live in a Time that hath rendered some kind of Frailties so habitual, that they lay Claim to large Grains of Allowance . . . our Sex seemeth to play the Tyrant in distinguishing partially for ourselves, by making that in the utmost degree Criminal in the Woman, which in a Man passeth under a much gentler Censure. The Root and Excuse of this Injustice" is, he tells her, "the Preservation of Families", and by having this in her keeping she is more than recompensed. And then we come to her own conduct if married to such a husband. "Remember", he tells her, "that next to the Danger of committing the Fault yourself, the greatest is that of seeing it in your Husband. Affected Ignorance which is seldom a Vertue is a great one here." Anything like "undecent

Complaint" will only end in making her "the reigning Jest". But, as he has promised to do, he points out the advantages that she may derive from the situation. This fault in a husband, he says, "will naturally make him more yielding in other Things", and with a hope that her admirable behaviour will at last convert him, he closes this section.

The next case which Lord Halifax considers seems to trouble him more. Elizabeth may be provided with a husband who loves wine "more than is convenient". "To fall upon the worst Side of a Drunkard, giveth so unpleasant a Prospect that it is not possible to dwell upon it. Let us pass then to the more favourable part, as far as a wife is concerned in it." One consolation that he thinks of is this: "in the first Place it will be no new Thing if you should have a Drunkard for a Husband". And again, there is another cheering thing to be said: "A Husband without Faults is a dangerous Observer; he hath an Eye so piercing, and seeth every Thing so plain, that it is exposed to the full Censure. . . . Thus in case a Drunken Husband should fall to your Share, if you will be wise and patient, his Wine shall be on your Side; it will throw a Veil over your Mistakes." Wisely received when he comes home, no storm, no reproaching look, and "the Wine will naturally work out all in Kindness, which a Wife must encourage, let it be wrapped up in never so much Impertinence". Elizabeth, he continues, will get more power and more credit in the family than if she had a husband who never put himself "into an Incapacity of holding the Reins".

And with a regret that you cannot, in spite of these alleviations, make drunkenness a virtue, "nor a Husband given to it a Felicity", Elizabeth is advised as to her conduct, if she should have chosen for her "a Cholerick or Ill-humoured Husband". In this case, "by marking how the Wheels of such a Man's Head are used to move, you may easily bring over all his Passion to your Party". Such a man, he tells her, who is "angry one day without any Sense, will the next Day be as kind without Reason". She should dexterously yield every thing, "till he beginneth to cool and then by slow Degrees you may rise and gain upon him". In this instance "a little Flattery may be admitted, which by being necessary will cease to be Criminal".

Having considered and dismissed these three cases, Lord Halifax presents a case which he seems to consider even more serious. "If in the Lottery of the World you should draw a Covetous Husband, I confess it will not make you proud of your good Luck." "The Complaint is now so general against all Husbands, that it giveth great Suspicion of its being ill-founded." But if we admit the worst, and her husband is really "a Close-handed Wretch", she must in this, as in other cases, endeavour to make it less afflicting to herself. Choose, he advises, seasonable hours for speaking; "a wise Friend" or "a third Hand", he says, "may often prevail more than you will be allowed to do in your own Cause".

When Lord Halifax deals with the supposition that his much-loved daughter might marry a feeble-minded husband we see to what a point acceptance of existing evils could then lead an enlightened and kindly father. "Such a one", he admits, "leaveth Room for a great many Objections." But God Almighty, in this case, too, has provided "a Remedy, or at least such a Mitigation as taketh away a great Part of the Sting and Smart of it". This "Mitigation" is: "that a Wife very often maketh a better Figure, for her Husband's making no great one". She must set against the grief that this "unseasonable weakness" may give her, the fact that this weakness giveth her the "Dominion".

After this Lord Halifax does, for about twenty lines, give rein to his fancy and describes the kind of husband she is "to pray for". I cannot think that he had great hope that her prayers would be answered, for he gives this husband but scant attention, and the most attractive thing that he can say about him is that he, knowing how to be master, "for that very reason will not let you feel the Weight of it". Even if Elizabeth's prayers were answered, one could hardly call marriage with a man, whose chief recommendation is that he will not make it too clear that he is the master, what Steele called "a case of Friendship". Steele's ideal never seems to have entered Lord Halifax's mind. In her future life his daughter may look forward to loving her children—even her servants may be humble friends—but her husband is to be watched, bamboozled, and "gained upon".

Lord Halifax, who has so much to say that his little book would grow into a volume, unsuitable for a New Year's gift, if he said it all, does not end on this note. After all this unworthy and ungenerous wisdom he shows again, in a touching passage, the deep affection that was the motive of this astonishing revelation of his views. Among her husband's friends, he tells her, she may be treated as "an unlawful invader", and he advises her: "That you would, as much as Nature will give you leave, endeavour to forget the great Indulgence you have found at Home. . . . The Tenderness we have had for you, My Dear, is of another Nature, peculiar to kind Parents, and differing from that which you will meet with first in any Family into which you shall be transplanted. . . ." But, after all, he says, there is a hope, for, "when you are used to it, you may like the House you go to better than that you left". And he adds, in words stamped with affection and sincerity: "As well as we love you, we shall yield up all Competition."

Lord Halifax made a great match for his daughter. The husband that his "care and experience" provided for Elizabeth, when she was nineteen, was the third Earl of Chesterfield. Of him his son's biographer, W. E. Browning, says: "Little more need be told than that he was a man of morose disposition and violent passions"; and his famous son, the fourth Earl, writes of his own education, and says: "My father was neither desirous nor able to advise me." We have scant knowledge of Elizabeth's life after her marriage, but we know that she had four sons and two daughters, and that she died while her eldest son, the writer of the *Letters*, was still a child. She died too young to take advantage of the best part of her father's advice—that which concerned her relations with her children when in their turn their wits began to "sprout".

Lord Halifax's love for his daughter is infectious, and we who read about her to-day do not wonder that he shrank "as if he were struck" when he thought of the dangers to which she would be so soon exposed. What we do wonder at is that his love stopped short at warning, that his philosophy advised nothing but submission, and that it never occurred to his active and sceptical mind that the legal and social position of women could be changed.

LOCKE'S FRIEND, LADY MASHAM

CHAPTER III

LOCKE'S FRIEND, LADY MASHAM

DAMARIS MASHAM, second wife of Sir Francis Masham, Bart., and friend of John Locke, was born in 1658. She was the daughter of Ralph Cudworth, Regius Professor of Hebrew at Cambridge for the forty-three eventful years from 1645 to his death in 1688. Cudworth had been the leader of the Cambridge Platonists, and was, like most of his followers, in political sympathy with the Cromwellians. He was an unusually open-minded controversialist. In the preface to a sermon preached before the House of Commons in 1647 he did not spare the men with whom he sympathized and who were then at the height of political power. He insists on the need of a spirit among Christians that we cannot "inclose in words and letters". And in another place he says that Christians should not content themselves "with the mere holding of right and Orthodox opinions". "I fear that many of us that pull down Idols in Churches may set them up in our Hearts." When he wrote on the existence of God he was said by Dryden to have put his opponents' case so forcibly, and raised "such strong objections against the being of a God and Providence that many think he hath not answered them".

Damaris Masham was therefore brought up in a home in which mental independence was valued as well as scholarship. Her name, however, would be unknown to-day, if it were not that her friendship with John Locke had important consequences, not only for the friends themselves, but for the whole world. The Cudworths knew Locke in 1682, when Damaris was twenty-three, just before Locke's seven years of exile in Holland. Damaris and her mother met him in London, probably at the house of their common friend Edward Clarke, husband of Locke's cousin, and afterwards M.P. for Taunton. For Clarke's guidance in the bringing up of his son, Locke, while he was in Holland, wrote the letters which are the original draft of his *Thoughts concerning Education*. "My first acquaintance with him", Lady Masham wrote after Locke's death, "began when he was past the middle age of man and I but young. . . . I had for a great part of above two years conversed freely with him, and he favoured me sometimes with his correspondence in Holland."[1] In 1685, when Locke had been three years in Holland, Damaris Cudworth was married to Francis Masham, and became the step-mother of nine children; and a year after her marriage her only son, Francis Cudworth Masham, was born.

At the revolution of 1688 Locke came home, a man of fifty-nine. He lived in London, and though threatened with consumption, was deeply engaged in public affairs. For a year or two he was a frequent and much-loved guest of Sir Francis and Lady Masham at Oates, their home in Essex; and from 1691 until his

[1] *Locke and Clarke* (Rand), 1927, p. 13.

death fourteen years later he lived at Oates. Ballard, in his *Memoirs of Learned Ladies* (1752), says of Lady Masham that "Mr. Locke was a domestic in her family many years". But the real nature of the arrangement is known to us from the letter written by Lady Masham to Le Clerc after Locke's death. She tells him that Mr. Locke had "obliged" Sir Francis and herself by long visits at Oates, and that he found the air of London increasingly trying to his health. He would not, however, consent to live at Oates until Sir Francis and Lady Masham had agreed to let him make an arrangement to defray his own expenses. He had, she writes, "all the assurances we could give him of being always welcome here; but, to make him easy in living with us, it was necessary he should do so on his own terms, which Sir Francis at last consenting to, Mr. Locke then believed himself to be at home with us, and resolved, if it pleased God, here to end his days—as he did".[1]

Locke's letters give us some glimpses of Damaris Masham's life and thoughts at Oates. She showed, he says, great eagerness to hear all about Limborch, because she remembered the correspondence he had had formerly with her father. Locke says, in writing to the Earl of Pembroke on Freemasonry in 1696: "Most of the notes . . . are what I made yesterday for my Lady Masham, who is become so fond of masonry as to say that she now more than ever wishes

[1] MS. in the Remonstrants' Library, Amsterdam, quoted in Fox Bourne's *Life of Locke*, Vol. I, p. 47.

herself a man that she might be capable of admission into the fraternity." In March 1690–91, shortly after he came to live at Oates, Locke wrote to Limborch a careful description of her mind. "The lady is so well versed in theological and philosophical studies, and of such an original mind, that you will not find many men to whom she is not superior in wealth of knowledge and ability to profit by it. Her judgement is excellent, and I know few who can bring such clearness of thought to bear upon the most abstruse subjects, or such capacity for searching through and solving the difficulties of questions beyond the range, I do not say of most women, but even of most learned men."

It was from Lady Masham that Locke's friends and fellow-workers gathered information about him after his death, and they echoed his respect for her. Le Clerc, in his *Eloge historique de Mr. Locke*, while speaking of Lady Masham as a worthy daughter of one of the greatest men of his time, says simply: "Cette illustre Dame . . . a eu le tems de connoître Mr. Locke à fond, pendant qu'il a été chez elle; comme elle est parfaitement capable de juger des gens, les lumières que j'ai reçues d'elle me serviront beaucoup à faire le portrait de ce Grand Homme." In the article which appeared shortly after Locke's death in *Nouvelles de la République des Lettres* for February 1705, the writer speaks of Lady Masham as a lady "pour qui Mr. Locke avoit conçu depuis longtems une amitié toute particulière". He then adds: "Malgré tout le mérite de cette dame, elle n'aura aujourd'hui de moi que cette louange." Locke and his friends were men who weighed their words.

Life in the purer air of Oates did not prevent the growth of Locke's lung trouble. Even in 1689 he writes that sometimes, after a little movement, he has not breath to speak, and that he "cannot borrow an hour or two of watching from the night without repaying it with a great waste of time the next day". And some years later he says: "The flattery of my summer vigour ought not to make me count beyond the next winter at any time for the future. The last sat so heavy on me, that it was with difficulty I got through it." But in despite of Locke's health these were years for him of splendid public service, of literary production, and of friendship with men who were doing the intellectual work of Europe. He published while at Oates the essay on the "Liberty of the Press", which has permanently influenced public feeling both in England and America. He took the initiative in reforming the currency after the financial confusion of two revolutions. He prepared for the press his *Thoughts concerning Education* (1693); and from 1696 he held the arduous post of Commissioner of the Board of Trade.

The *Essay concerning Human Understanding*—the book "begun", he says, "by chance, and continued by entreaty"; the book which he hoped might be useful "in clearing the ground a little and removing some of the rubbish that lies in the way to knowledge";[1] the

[1] Fox Bourne, *Life of Locke*, Vol. II, p. 135.

book which shook the world, and for whose copyright Locke received thirty pounds—had been published in the spring before he went to live at Oates. The *Essay* involved him in a series of controversies, and at Oates he prepared the later editions. But he found time for friendship with Lady Masham's charming young step-daughter, Esther Masham, and he acted as medical adviser to old Mrs. Cudworth, who since her husband's death had lived with the Mashams. He advised Lady Masham in her own studies as well as in the education of her little boy. All this was only made possible by the healthy life and sympathetic atmosphere of the house at Oates. There can have been few country houses at the end of the seventeenth century where the importance of the work Locke was doing would have been so truly estimated, or where his friendship would have been so deeply valued.

Mrs. Cudworth died in November 1695. Locke and Clarke were trustees under her will, and a series of difficulties arose, of the kind which too often produce bitter family quarrels. A sum of about £500 seems to have been left in trust for Lady Masham and her son. That sum had to be collected from her brother and her husband, both of whom showed themselves dilatory and unbusiness-like in the matter. Locke's letters to Clarke from Oates prove that he and Lady Masham acted both patiently and firmly. On January 26, 1697, Locke writes that he hopes "the business between her and her brother is now in a way to an end",[1]

[1] *Locke and Clarke* (Rand), p. 497.

VIEW OF OATES, ESSEX

thanks, in part, to a letter in which Lady Masham had "seconded" a letter from the Bishop of Gloucester, "and explained it, so as to make it", Locke thinks, "more intelligible and of more force". The negotiations with Sir Francis Masham were more difficult. Sir Francis insisted that his personal bond was sufficient security, although it would bear no interest, and might, in case of his death, be difficult to collect. The trustees, on behalf of Lady Masham and her son, required a mortgage on some part of his estate. The correspondence carried on through Clarke might be used as a model of the way in which three wise people can deal with an obstinate man without either surrendering their rights or forcing a quarrel.

There were frequent, and always welcome, visits at Oates from Edward Clarke's children—Edward, the first of the boys on whom Locke's theories of education were tried, and Elizabeth, the little girl whom Locke always referred to as "my wife". Locke also sent suggestions to his new friend Molyneux, who as soon as they became friends confided to him on March 2, 1693, his anxiety over the bringing up of his motherless son, at this time only four years old. Molyneux, who was trying to be both father and mother to the child, as to whom he admits that his "affections are strongly placed on him", shows a pathetic eagerness for the appearance of Locke's *Thoughts concerning Education*. Locke's reply, on March 28th, is characteristic. "Your impatience to see them, has not, I assure you, slack-

F

ened my hand". So that, while Locke was preparing his *Thoughts concerning Education* for the press, he was giving educational advice to three families, and was able to watch the effect of that advice on children all but one of whom he knew personally. A comparison of the successive editions of the *Thoughts* shows Locke's mind constantly at work on the experience and criticisms of his friends. On November 16, 1695, he writes to Molyneux: "I am glad you approve of the additions to the third Edition of my *Education*; you are a Father, and are concerned not to be deceived, and therefore I expect you will not flatter me in this point."

It is difficult to realize the part which fear then played in the bringing up of children. There are, in the literature of that time, many more sensational accounts of its effect on a child's mind, but none more impressive than that contained in a long and interesting passage in the *Thoughts concerning Education* which does not appear in the first edition, and was probably due to reflection started by the suggestions of his friends. "I believe there is nobody that reads this, but may recollect what disorder hasty or imperious words from his parents or teachers have caused in his thoughts; how for the time it has turned his brains so that he scarce knew what was said by or to him" (*Ed.*, p. 188).[1] Again and again Locke emphasizes the commonness of this trouble. "Instances," he writes, "of such who in a weak

---

[1] I refer to the *Thoughts concerning Education* as "Ed.", with the pages of the edition of 1800.

timorous mind, have borne, all their whole lives through, the effects of a fright when they were young are everywhere to be seen" (*Ed.*, p. 129). With a psychological insight far ahead of his time he drives home the futility rather than the cruelty of such methods. Parents and governors, he says, should "not make themselves such scarecrows that their scholars should always tremble in their sight. . . . It is as impossible to draw fair and regular characters on a trembling mind, as on a shaking paper" (*Ed.*, p. 189). But affection will out, and some of Locke's most vigorous passages are aimed against the fantastic indulgence that was so often combined with this treatment. He finds it necessary to give even the enlightened people of his day, in his *Thoughts concerning Education*, a serious warning against allowing children to "be used to strong drink, especially to sit up late at night taking drink in private with the servants" (*Ed.*, p. 23). From a modern point of view Locke's own advice is marred by his constant anxiety lest, if a child once gets the upper hand, his character may be ruined. Both in his book and his letters to Clarke he recommends that, if whipping has to be resorted to, it should be given in a severe measure, to "master stubbornness" (*Ed.*, p. 78). But he disliked the idea of corporal punishment so much that he gave the whole energy of his mind to advocating such a treatment of children of tender years that it should never be necessary to appeal to it.

Locke's modesty never slept, and it sometimes led

him to underestimate fantastically the value of his work. Still, he is right when he tells us that his *Thoughts concerning Education* contains no systematic scheme. And yet, in spite of repetitions and inconsistencies, his general attitude to the mind of a little child must have brought the relief of daylight to Damaris Masham and Mr. Molyneux, both of whom were "tender parents" of only sons. His description of the respect and courtesy with which the natural curiosity of a child should be treated cannot be improved on to-day. Children are, he says, "Travellers newly arrived in a strange country, of which they know nothing; we should therefore make conscience not to mislead them. . . . And happy are they who meet with civil people, that will comply with their ignorance and help them to get out of it" (*Ed.*, pp. 139–140). "The native and untaught suggestions of inquisitive children do often offer things that may set a considering man's thoughts on work. And I think there is frequently more to be learnt from the unexpected questions of a child, than the discourses of men, who talk in a road, according to the notions they have borrowed, and the prejudices of their education" (*Ed.*, pp. 140–141).

A genuine difficulty that then confronted parents was the crushing nature of the formalities demanded from children. One breath of Locke's good sense blew most of this trouble away. He points out that neither "a ploughman" nor your son will be "more polite" in his language and carriage "than those he uses to converse with". And of the "putting off of their hats, and making legs" modishly (*Ed.*, p. 165), he declared that they should not be much troubled about it. He is, on the whole, against the buying of toys for children. "If you will help a child make things it will more endear you to them than any chargeable toys you shall buy them" (*Ed.*, p. 150). It is pleasing, however, in his early accounts, to find more than one entry of this kind, "1/6 for drum for little T." There is one passage in the *Thoughts concerning Education* which Molyneux—and, as he assures Locke, others—"stumbled at". Locke's advice, "that a child should never be suffered to have what he craves, or so much as speaks for, much less if he cries for it" (*Ed.*, p. 112), seemed to Mr. Molyneux (August 12, 1693) "to bear hard on the tender Spirits of Children and the Natural Affections of Parents". Molyneux, from the point of view of a father, speaks of the difficulty it would be for any person "to study the unaccountable Fancy and Diversion of Children, the whole Year round". And again, of its "racking the invention of any living man to find employment for them". Locke in his not very consistent answer of August 23rd satisfies his friend that he was not against children following their harmless fancies and desires.

Molyneux set to work, with the same keenness that Lady Masham had shown, to educate his son on Locke's principles; Locke (July 2, 1695) asks Molyneux particularly to let him know the results of the method on his little boy. "I should be glad", he says, "to know the Particulars; for though I have seen the success of it in a child of the Lady in whose house I am, (whose Mother has taught him Latin without knowing it herself when she began) yet I would be glad to have other Instances; because some Men who cannot endure any Thing should be mended in the World by a new Method, object, I hear, that my Way of Education is impracticable." In another passage of the same letter Locke writes: "The Child above-mentioned [Francis Masham] but nine Years old in June last, has learnt to read and write very well; is now reading Quintus Curtius with his Mother, under-stands Geography and Chronology very well, and the Copernican System of our Vortex; is able to multiply well, and divide a little; and all without ever having one Blow for his Book."

In a passage in the *Thoughts concerning Education* not in the original letters to Clarke, he says: "Whatever stir there is about getting of Latin, as the great and difficult business, his Mother may teach it him her-self, if she will but spend two or three Hours in a Day with him and make him read the Evangelists in Latin to her. . . . I do not mention this, as an Imagination, of what I fancy may do, but as of a thing I have known done, and the Latin tongue with ease got this way" (*Ed.*, p. 205). It is pleasing to know that Molyneux's little boy's education was equally satisfactory, and that besides his proficiency in Latin and the globes his father could say of him at the age of five that he does not believe that "any Child had ever his Passions more perfectly at Command".

In physical matters Damaris Masham, when she set herself to follow Locke's advice, had a still harder task, for Locke tells Molyneux (August 23, 1693) that when he came to live at Oates, Francis, a boy of five and "the only son of a very tender Mother", was "almost destroyed by a too tender keeping". Locke advises, in his *Thoughts concerning Education*, hard beds; "for being burried every night in feathers melts and dissolves the body" (*Ed.*, p. 26). Children, he says, should rise early; their diet is to be so strict that, if possible, the very existence of such fruits as grapes and plums should be kept from them (*Ed.*, p. 23). Their shoes should be thin enough to leak and let in water (*Ed.*, p. 10). It must have needed some courage on Lady Masham's part to follow this advice. But however much we may disagree with this or that detail of Locke's system, he gave Francis Masham an out-of-door life and plenty of air, exercise, and sunshine, at a time when boys as well as girls were constantly kept in the "shade", on account of their complexions. Happily, when Francis is eight years old, Locke is able to tell Molyneux that "He is now by a contrary Usage come to bear Wind and Weather, and wet in his Feet; and the Cough which threatened him, under that warm and cautious Management, has left him, and is now no longer his Parents constant Apprehension as it was".

Of Francis Masham's later life we know little; but we have a glimpse of him in a letter which Locke wrote, when he was dying, to his cousin and heir, Peter

King. He says: "It is my earnest request to you to take care of the youngest son of Sir Francis and Lady Masham, in all his concerns as if he were your brother. He has never failed to pay me all the respect and to do me all the good offices he was capable of performing." Francis Masham must have had at least a touch of his Mother in his character, for Locke adds, "with all manner of cheerfulness and delight".[1]

I like to think of the many talks that must have taken place during these years at Oates, between the mother, with her intimate love and knowledge of her son, and Locke, with his wide experience and humanity, on the fundamental points of education. They will have agreed together, as we agree with Locke to-day, that "he that has found a way how to keep a child's spirits easy, active, and free, and yet at the same time to restrain him from many things he has a mind to, and to draw him to things that are uneasy to him; he, I say, that knows how to reconcile these seeming contradictions, has, in my opinion, got the true secret of education" (*Ed.*, pp. 43–44). Locke must have been thinking of Lady Masham when he speaks, in the last sentence of his *Thoughts concerning Education*, of those "whose concern for their dear little ones makes them so irregularly bold, that they dare venture to consult their own reason, in the education

---

[1] Fox Bourne, *Life of Locke*, Vol. II, p. 555. The Bishop of Durham, in the preface (p. xi) to Cudworth's *Treatise on Eternal Morality* (1731), says that the MS. belongs to "his grandson, Francis Cudworth Masham, Esq., one of the Masters in Chancery, whose temper is too beneficent and communicative" to keep it unpublished.

of their children, rather than wholly to rely upon old custom".

It was not only in matters of education that Damaris Masham's mind was "irregularly bold". In her whole life—domestic, social, and religious—she took reason as her guide. Two strong forces were against her. The first was the view of many sincere religious people of her time that the concerns of this world should be treated as dust and ashes, and all effort concentrated on preparation for the next. The other force, no less strong, but based on less worthy motives, was the social prejudice that opposed the spread of knowledge among women. The first of these forces can be best understood by studying a published appeal made to Lady Masham in 1690 by Mr. John Norris, Vicar of Bemerton, in a little book called *Reflections upon the Conduct of Human Life, in a letter to my Lady Masham*. The book is written on the assumption that Lady Masham has lost her sight, and is a sustained argument that, owing to the worthlessness of human knowledge, she need not regret this loss.

Mr. Norris had been a follower of Damaris Masham's father. After he left Oxford he took a country living, married and had thirteen children, a conviction of the worthlessness of mundane life and learning growing upon him all the while. He wrote many books, among them a work on *Christian Blessedness*, one on *Christian Prudence*, and another on *The Grossness of the Quaker Principle of the Light within*. Women listened to him eagerly, and for many

hundreds of people, troubled by the new ideas that
were gaining ground, he stood as a bulwark against
the dangerous doctrines of Quakers, Socinians, and
Atheists. He enjoyed correspondence with learned
ladies. Mary Astell was touched by his interest in her
ideas. She writes: "Hitherto I have courted Truth with
a kind of Romantic Passion, in spite of all Difficulties
and Discouragements, for knowledge is thought so
unnecessary an accomplishment for a Woman that
few will give themselves the trouble to assist them in
the Attainment of it. . . . But now, since you have so
generously put into my hand an Opportunity of
obtaining what I so greedily long after . . . I give
myself up entirely to your Conduct so far as is consistent with a rational not blind obedience."[1] People
brought him all manner of difficulties. In his *Miscellanies* there is an answer to a gentleman who wants to
know whether friendship is possible between a man
and his wife. Mr. Norris discusses this point at length.
In conclusion he says: "I think I may now from the
Premises venture to affirm, that there may be strict
Friendship between Man and Wife." It is true, he
argues, that there is not equality, which in most cases
is necessary for friendship, but, he says, a husband
like "the greatest Monarch in the World may find
Opportunities to descend from the Throne of Majesty
to the familiar Caresses of a dear Favourite: and
unking himself a while for the more glorious Title of
Friend" (4th edition, pp. 372–373).

[1] John Norris, *Letters concerning the Love of God* (1695), p. 78.

In 1691 Mr. Molyneux lit on the *Reflections upon the Conduct of Human Life*, and wrote to Locke about it, sending a message of sympathy to Lady Masham on the loss of her eyesight. Locke, in his reply, tells Molyneux that Lady Masham begs him to say that she is not blind, and that in proof of this she hopes to *see* Mr. Molyneux at Oates in the summer. Locke also tells Molyneux that Lady Masham had sent a message to Mr. Norris to tell him that she had not lost her sight, but that Mr. Norris, "having fitted his Epistle to that supposition, could not be hindered from publishing it". She has, he says further, "but weak eyes, which Mr. Norris, for reasons he knows best, was resolved to make blind ones". Mr. Molyneux replies to this: "I ever looked on Mr. Norris as an obscure Enthusiastic Man, but I could not think he would knowingly impose on the world so notorious a falsity in matter of fact."

Although Locke and Molyneux did not think Mr. Norris's *Reflections upon the Conduct of Human Life* worth their serious attention, it is of interest to us to-day, both because it puts with force and clearness the point of view against which Lady Masham's whole life was a protest, and because it gives us, from a less admiring friend than Locke, a confirmation of his estimate of the powers of her mind. Locke tells Molyneux that Lady Masham has been a great reader. Mr. Norris, in his dedication, says: "The chief reason why your Ladyship is so concerned for the loss of your Sight, is because you are thereby deprived of Conversation with your books and consequently retarded in your earnest pursuit after Learning and Knowledge." Of her scholarship he says that "the two great masters in the study of truth are Descartes and Malebranche, of both of which your Ladyship is so much a Mistress" (ibid., p. 62) that, he argues, it is needless for her to know more. He says that she has the curious effect on him of making him "brief". "Did not the quickness of your Ladyship's Apprehension oblige me to Brevity I could be Voluminous" (ibid., p. 111). And again: "I know your Ladyship loves to have something left to *work out* by yourself in your own private Meditations. Which Consideration had made me all along use less Prolixity than the Quaintness and Weightiness of my Argument would otherwise justifie" (ibid., p. 72). To anyone who has even looked into Mr. Norris's other works, no direct compliment to Lady Masham's mind could be as impressive as these words.

In the book itself, which, thanks to her, is of moderate length, Mr. Norris follows the division of knowledge familiar to the students of his time, into "necessary" and "contingent". "Necessary" knowledge only includes those sciences "antecedent to the present world" and which might have been studied before it was made. He argues that Lady Masham with her "quickness of understanding" will be easily persuaded that to grasp subjects that did not begin with our "mutable system", eyesight is not required. It is true that to master "contingent" subjects you need it, but for these subjects Mr. Norris has scant respect. He speaks of history as an attempt to know "what a company of silly Creatures, call'd men, have been doing for almost this 6000 years" (ibid., p. 45). He is eloquent when he thinks of the time wasted on "Tongues". "Never certainly," he says, "was there a grosser piece of Idolatry . . . to place Learning in that, which is one of the greatest Curses upon Earth, and which shall utterly Cease in Heaven" (ibid., p. 44). Natural science fares no better in his hands. "And yet," he says, "is there anything more Absurd and Impertinent—than to have a Man, who has so great a Concern upon his Hands as the Preparing for Eternity, all busie and taken up with Quadrants, and Telescopes, Furnaces, Syphons and Air-Pumps?" (ibid., p. 132). Why then, he repeats, should Lady Masham regret that she has lost her sight?

Locke and Lady Masham were right in seeing danger to all constructive human effort in this counsel of despair, and yet in his criticism of the existing educational methods and his honest anger against the waste of time at the Universities, Mr. Norris is not unlike Locke, and the sincerity of his feelings gives poignancy to his phrases.

In the same little book he says: "Nothing but Read, Read, as long as Eyes and Spectacles will last, not regarding whether the Head be Clear, so that it be full" (ibid., p. 96). " 'Tis then only they Study, when they are hanging their Heads over an old Musty Folio, and are making huge Common-places [i.e. books of extracts] and stuffing their Memories with Grey

Sentences and Venerable Sayings" (ibid., p. 94). Such "unedifying stuffage of the mind" does not lead to thought, and yet "the first Inventors of Arts and Sciences . . . made their way into the Coasts of Learning by meer dint of Thinking" (ibid., p. 49).

Norris tells Lady Masham that he spent about thirteen years "in the most celebrated university in the world . . . according to the ordinary measures perhaps not amiss" (ibid., p. 157). And yet he feels that he has as much to answer for in giving so large a part of his days to "unconcerning curiosities" as he has in the moral weaknesses of his youth. Those thirteen years were just so much lost time. After death, when "we enjoy the Beatific vision we shall commence instantaneously Wise and Learned, and be fully possess'd of the Tree of Knowledge as well as of the Tree of Life". He pleads from cover to cover with Damaris Masham to follow him, and to give up "unconcerning curiosities". He himself, he tells her, intends to spend the "uncertain remainder" of his time in chiefly applying himself to the reading of such books "as are rather Persuasive, than Instructive, such as are sapid, Pathetic and Divinely-Relishing, such as Warm, Kindle and inlarge the Interior" (ibid., p. 158).

In 1696 a little book appeared, *A Discourse concerning the Love of God*. It was published anonymously, but was soon known to be by Lady Masham. It is not a direct answer to Mr. Norris's appeal and warning to her in his *Reflections upon the Conduct of Human Life*. Between the dates of Norris's *Reflections* and Damaris Masham's

Discourse, Locke's *Reasonableness of Christianity* had been published anonymously, and also Mr. Norris's correspondence with Mary Astell on the Love of God; and Mr. Norris, in the fourth edition of his *Practical Discourses on Divinity*, had replied to his critics.

Lady Masham's book is her share in this whole controversy, and it shows her a clear and ardent exponent of Locke's views. Her chief point is that Mr. Norris's view, largely derived from his great master, Malebranche, disparages Christianity by asserting "that it unfits men for Society" (*D.*, p. 122)[1]. For her, as for Locke, the cultivation of the powers of the mind is not only not inconsistent with Christianity, but is in fact an essential part of it. If, she writes, we are to have, as Mr. Norris maintains, "no Desires but after God, the several Societies of Mankind could not long hold together, nor the very species be continued" (*D.*, p. 83).

She is not troubled, as Mary Astell was, about the question whether the "Love of the Creature should exclude the Love of God; any more than that the Love of Cherries should exclude the love of our Friend that gives them us" (*D.*, p. 88). Even flowers had their place in her scheme of things. "For, as short-liv'd Flowers, tho' they ought not to imploy the continual care of our whole lives, may yet reasonably enough be found in our Gardens, and delight us in

---

[1] I refer to Lady Masham's *Discourse concerning the Love of God* (1696) as "D.", and to her *Occasional Thoughts in reference to a Vertuous or Christian Life* (1694) as "O."

their Seasons; So the fading Good Things of this Life, tho' (for that reason) they are not to be fixed on as the Ultimate Good of Eternal Beings, yet there is no reason why we may not rejoice in them, as the good Gifts of God, and find all that Delight which he has joined with the lawful use of them" (D., p. 99). She tries to show Mr. Norris where she thinks that his arguments should lead him. He ought, she says, according to his theories, to conclude with Malebranche that the right thing to do would be to give himself the happiness of attending eternity in "Desarts". And she hits a man with thirteen children and a country living rather hard when she suggests that he "has no inclination to this way of Living, and that it is to that that we owe his Happy Invention of Seeking and injoying the good things of the World without loving them" (D., p. 124).

In this book Lady Masham was defending the life of reason against religious theory. The great interest of her second book, *Occasional Thoughts in reference to a Vertuous or Christian Life* (1694), is that she there defends the rational life against social prejudice. She saw, as Mary Astell and all the serious women of her time saw, that such prejudices had their greatest influence in preventing the education of girls, and that an enlightened social and home life was not possible without the co-operation of educated women. Lady Masham tells us that the idea of her second book came to her from a conversation that took place some years before at Oates. She says: "Those persons who

afforded that agreeable Conversation I have mentioned were, the greater part of them Ladies"; and, "it
was not strange if they express'd much displeasure at
the too general neglect of the Instruction of their
Sex". And then from considering "the miscarriage
and unhappiness of Mankind in general", the whole
conversation terminated "in a more peculiar Consideration of that part which those of their own
Condition had in the one and the other" (*O.*, pp. 8, 9).

This "peculiar consideration" is the part of her
book which tells us most of Damaris Masham's character and of the social conditions of her day. In it she
develops no scheme of education for girls, and she
does not even refer to Mary Astell's idea of a College,
of which she must have known, but of which from
the difference of their opinions on religious matters
she was certainly distrustful. But from her own knowledge and observation she confirms all that others
have said on the state of ignorance in which the girls
of the well-to-do classes then lived, and the difficulties before anyone who advocated a change.
"Girls," she tells us, "betwixt silly Fathers and
ignorant Mothers, are generally so brought up that
traditionary Opinions are to them, all their lives long,
instead of Reason" (*O.*, p. 162). A real grasp of the
principles of religion was to her an essential part of
education, but she says girls are supposed to have
"learnt the Principles of Religion when their Nurses,
or Maids, Taught them their Catechisms" (*O.*, p. 18).
"The greater part among ourselves are instructed in

G

Religion much after the same manner that that good
Lady of the Church of Rome instructed her Child;
who when the Girl told her, she could not believe
Transubstantiation; Reply'd, What? You are a
naughty Girl, and must be whip'd" (*O.*, p. 39). It is,
then, no wonder if "a Habit of Idleness or Inapplica-
tion of the Mind be got, which once contracted is very
hardly cur'd" (*O.*, p. 193). She points out: "Women do
the most inevitably suffer as not having the like
Advantage (at least early enough) of Correcting the
Ignorance, or Errors of their Child-hood that Men
have." She agrees with La Bruyère that "Men have
made no Laws, or put out any Edicts whereby Women
are prohibited to open their Eyes; to Read, to Remember what they Read and to make use thereof in their
Conversation, or in composing of Works" (*O.*, p. 201).
But "M. Bruyère" must know that it is not only
"edicts" that can restrain a woman from learning.
"It is sufficient for this that no body assists them in it;
and that they are made to see betimes that it would
be disadvantageous to them to have it" (*O.*, p. 202).

Parents, she admits, may well shrink from educating
their girls, "from an apprehension that should their
Daughters be perceiv'd to understand any Learned
Language, or be conversant in Books, they might be
in danger of not finding Husbands: so few Men, as
do, relishing these accomplishments in a Lady" (*O.*,
p. 197). She appeals to the girls themselves not to let
the laughter of "wits" prevent them acquiring through
books, in their home life, all the knowledge possible,

as she had done in her own girlhood in Cambridge.
"Ladies would do well", she writes, "if before they
came to the care of Families they did imploy some of
their many idle Hours in gaining a little Knowledge
in Languages, and the useful Sciences" (*O.*, p. 192).
Lady Masham urges this because she believed, with
Locke, that after marriage it was important that a
mother should be able to educate her own children in
their early years, boys as well as girls. Boys, as Locke
had shown, through the unwillingness of fathers to
spend enough money on education to secure good
tutors, had nothing to look forward to but weary
years of classical scholarship, unwillingly learnt by
the help of blows, and rapidly forgotten. Lady
Masham concentrates her thoughts on the very young
children whom Locke had advised mothers to teach
themselves. "Whoso", she says, "has try'd how very
little Sense is to be met with, or can be infus'd into
Nurses and Nursemaids and with what difficulty
. . . will soon be satisfy'd how little fit it is to trust
children any more than is necessary in such Hands"
(*O.*, pp. 184–185). "For the Teaching of little Children
so as not to disgust them, does require much greater
Patience and Address, than Common People are often
capable of; or than most can imagine, who have not
experience hereof" (*O.*, p. 194).

Locke, when he urged parents to spend their money
on engaging good tutors, had said: "Spare it in toys
and play-games, in silk and ribbons, laces, and other
useless expences, as much as you please. . . . It is

not good husbandry to make his fortune rich, and his mind poor." Lady Masham points out that it must not be assumed that every parent can spend large sums on tuition, and that it is "a thing practicable but by a very few to purchase the having always Wise, vertuous and well Bred People to take the place of a Parent in governing their Children", and that money is not the only difficulty: "for the World", she says, "does not abound with such Persons as these" (O., p. 187). So, inadequately equipped as the mothers of families are to be teachers, it is well for them to take up this work. She appeals quite simply as a lady of quality to other ladies of quality, "since", she says, "the Relation between the Mother and Child is equal amongst all Ranks of People. And it is a very preposterous Abuse of Quality to make it a pretence for being unnatural" (O., p. 177). Her common sense, and perhaps her full acceptance of Locke's views, carries her farther. "No one", she adds, "is born into the World to live idly; enjoying the Fruit and Benefit of other People's Labours without contributing reciprocally some way or other to the good of the Community" (O., p. 179).

Boys suffered not only from the dullness of the classical schools, but also from their narrowness. Even a self-educated mother could create in her son an interest in subjects essential for his future life but wholly ignored in the schools and colleges of the time. Damaris Masham, we learn from her second book, had found that the young country squires were so educated as to have no insight "into the law which they are to see executed, and into that Constitution which they are to support". History, Politics, and Morals are subjects, she writes, "which an English Gentleman cannot, without blame, be ignorant of"; and again, that a knowledge of these subjects is "essential to the duly Qualifying him for what is his proper business" (*O.*, pp. 170–171).

Lady Masham knows that it is not to be expected that men whose own education is so imperfect will welcome knowledge and education in their wives; and so she is led to consider the education of women, not only from the point of view of a mother's relation with her children, but in the relation of man and wife. She is one of those who think it "but Natural, and alike so in both Sexes, to desire to please the other. I may, I suppose, without any Injurious Reflection upon Ladies, presume, that if Men did usually find Women the more amiable for being knowing, they would much more commonly, than now they are, be so" (*O.*, p. 204).

Her own experience as a daughter and mother had shown her how community of mind helps the daily intercourse of men and women. Her view of marriage is a hopeful although not a modern one. Living in the seventeenth century she accepts without protest the fact that "The necessities of a Family very often, and the injustice of Parents sometimes, causes People to sacrifice their Inclinations, in this matter, to interest" (*O.*, pp. 215–16). But "even", she says, "if this State

is uneasy in the beginning . . . yet scarce any vertuous and reasonable Man and Woman who are
Husband and Wife, can know that it is both their
Duty and Interest (as it is) reciprocally to make each
other Happy without effectually doing so in a little
time". But where there is "no contrary inclination",
what happiness can there be like marriage? "Where
can Friendship the solidest and sweetest Pleasure in this
World . . . be maintained in its Perfection, as where
Two Persons have inseparably one and the same
Interest?" (*O.*, p. 216). But her experience is that
unhappiness in married life was all too common.
Marriage had become "a State almost as much fear'd
by the Wise, as dispis'd by Fools" (*O.*, p. 218). So
much so that, "one can frequent very little Company,
or know the Story of but few Families; without hearing
of the publick Divisions, and Discords of Marry'd
People, or learning their private Discontents from
their being in that state" (*O.*, p. 218).

Lady Masham dismisses, as worthy of only scant
attention, men who complain of their wives being
"expensive" and gaining admirers, while they themselves spend their time in "Drinking, Gaming, or
Lew'd Company. Such Persons of both Sexes as These,
are indeed but fit Scourges to chastise each other's
Folly" (*O.*, p. 214). Until there is a change in the
morals of the time, she sees no chance of a real increase
of happiness. What troubles her most is that it is the
married woman who is virtuous and sensitive who is
most often the unhappiest. Such a woman, "who

prefers her Husband's Affection to all things in the World" (*O.*, p. 226), is "the aptest to bear with an immoderate Grief, the ill-Humour, or unkindness of her Husband" (*O.*, p. 223). She does not hope "to persuade such whose Heads are full of pleasure and whose Hours pass gaily", but she says: "They who are wretched one would think, should be easily prevail'd with to hearken to any Proposition, which brings but the least glimpse of Happiness to them" (*O.*, p. 221). Lady Masham sees no easy way to make things better, though she believes that Mr. Locke's plan of a woman's educating her own children would do a great deal to make their lives less miserable. She believes that "in that division of Cares of Human Life, which ought to be made between a Man and his Wife" (*O.*, p. 190), "The Author of Nature" intended that the minds of children, as well as their bodies, should be a woman's especial care.

Lord Halifax, in his *Advice* to his loved daughter, recommends with all his force an acceptance of things as they are, combined with a readiness to enjoy any alleviation that offers itself. Lady Masham writes in the hope that, although there is no perfect solution, a better way of life is possible if men and women will but follow reason. Even those women who "have more Vertue than to think of returning the injuries they receive" must not give way "to a fruitless grief". Such a grief, she tells them, "renders them yet less agreeable to those whom they desire to please; and useless in the World". She knows that "constant ill-health and

diseases are the almost never failing Effects of a lasting Discontent upon such feeble Constitutions" (*O.*,
p. 224). Rational women, in whatever circumstances,
should employ their time better than "in the indulging
to a weakness very incident to tender Minds, which is
to bemoan themselves instead of casting about for
Relief against their Afflictions". She, one of the most
dutiful of women, begs women to have the "wit" to
show contempt for unkindness, and not "foolishly
sacrifice their Lives, or the Comforts of them (which
is our All in this World) to those who will not sacrifice
the least inclination to their reasonable Satisfaction"
(*O.*, p. 223). It is still open to them to have the real
joy of their children's well-being and affection. Their
husbands may treat them ill, but they can have
children who will honour and love their mothers "as
those to whom they owe much more than their Being".
She feels as a mother towards children, and finds it
very strange that women, "who resent with the deepest
Compassion every little Malady which afflicts their
Bodies", do not make an effort to help their children
in their studies, "from a Principle of Pitty to that
tender age" (*O.*, pp. 191–192).

But it is not only from the child's point of view that
she sees this question; it is perhaps the women themselves who are her chief concern. Apart from the good
that they can do to their children, women should
acquire "Ingenious Knowledge whereby they might
delightfully employ themselves". A woman, she
believes, "is but very ill provided to bear Discontent

. . . if she has nothing within her self which can afford her pleasure; independently upon others; Which is what none can lastingly have, without some improvement of their rational Faculties" (*O.*, p. 226). But a lady who would follow her advice must not hope for an easy task. She will "necessarily be oblig'd (for the gaining of Time wherein she might do so) to order the Course and Manner of her Life something differently from others of her Sex and Condition" (*O.*, p. 198). To do this will seem to convey a reproach to the idleness of other women, and she will be judged accordingly. If she lives in the town, the "wits" will consider her "as fit to be ridicul'd out of the World before others were infected by the example". She will be treated as a "Scare-crow", and many honest people will keep away from her house. "In the Country she would probably fare still worse; for there her understanding of the Christian Religion would go near to render her suspected of Heresy even by those who thought the best of her: Whilst her little Zeal for any Sect or Party would make the Clergy of all sorts give her out for a Socinian, or a Deist: And should but a very little Philosophy be added to her other Knowledge, even for an Atheist. The Parson of the Parish, for fear of being ask'd hard Questions, would be shy of coming near her, be his Reception ever so inviting." She must not hope to be visited by "such as Reverenc'd the Doctor". For, besides these reasons for avoiding her, the neighbourhood will "already be satisfy'd from the reports of Nurses, and Maids, that

their Lady was indeed a Woman of very odd Whim-
sies"; even though "her prudent Conduct and
Management of her Affairs would probably secure
her from being thought out of her Wits by her near
Neighbours" (O., pp. 199–200). In all this passage it
is clear that Lady Masham is thinking of herself and
her own life. There is no doubt that with her "little
Zeal for any Party or Sect" she must have been
accused of Socinianism, and that, as more than "a
little Philosophy" was added to her other knowledge,
she cannot have escaped the general gossip of the
vicarage and the servants' hall.

These passages were not written by Damaris
Masham to discourage other women, but to stiffen
their resolve to bring reason and knowledge into their
daily lives. She, one of the most reticent of women,
uses her personal experience in order that it may be
useful to others in the same difficulties. Of all this part
of her book her great master could not have written a
single word. The woman and scholar whom we have
learnt to know and to honour through the opinions of
others here begins to live for us in her own person.
Her conclusion is that "the Saving of but one Soul
from Destruction is a noble recompence for ten
Thousand such Censurers" (O., p. 200), such as she
has described, and must, in her life in Essex, have
suffered from.

Damaris Masham died in 1708. She was buried in
the middle aisle of Bath Abbey, and her epitaph, with
its statement that "she had the virtues of all classes",

reads like a real attempt to tell something of her character.

On September 30, 1692, shortly after Locke wrote to Limborch his famous eulogy of Lady Masham's mind, he wrote to Molyneux expressing his joy in his newly formed friendship with him. He says: "There are Beauties of the Mind as well of the Body, that take and prevail at first Sight: and, wherever I have met with this, I have readily surrender'd my self, and have never yet been deceiv'd in my Expectation." Locke's friendship with Damaris Masham only ended with his death at Oates in 1704, and the end of his own long fight for tolerance and reason. In her, his fellow-worker and his pupil, he was not deceived.

MARY ASTELL

(1666–1731)

CHAPTER IV

MARY ASTELL
(1666–1731)

MARY ASTELL, the only daughter of Peter Astell, a merchant of Newcastle-on-Tyne, was born in the year 1666. It is believed that she came to London at the age of twenty-two, and that she settled at once in Chelsea, where she lived till her death in 1731. In 1694 she published *A Serious Proposal to the Ladies for the Advancement of their True and Greatest Interest*, followed by a Second Part in 1697. This book was the first considered attempt to interest Englishwomen in the higher education of their sex. Mary Astell not only proposed to start what would have been the first English college for women, but she wrote about her project with convincing fervour, and was willing to devote to it all the powers of her fine mind. Ten thousand pounds were actually promised to her to make a beginning, by a lady who, we have reason to believe, was Queen Anne. But custom and prejudice were too strong. The great Bishop Burnet was alarmed. To his mind her scheme suggested a revival of the nunneries, and savoured of Rome.[1] The offer was withdrawn, and the women of England waited more than a century and a half before Bedford College, London, the first college "for the Advancement of their True and Greatest Interest", was established.

[1] *Mary Astell*, by Florence M. Smith, p. 23; and Ballard MSS. (Bodleian Library), xliii, 29.

Mary Astell's fame in her own day, and such recognition as she has been given in ours, have rested on the two Parts of her *Proposal*. But important as these were, it is only by a study of her other writings, and of the scanty materials for her life, that we can fully appreciate our debt to her. It was her "unwavering purpose" to improve the lot of those whom, in her dedication to the Princess Anne of the Second Part of the *Proposal*, she speaks as "the most neglected part of the World as to all Real improvement, the Ladies".

In Miss Florence M. Smith's scholarly and sympathetic monograph (Columbia University Press, 1916), Mary Astell stands out both as a pioneer in education and as a woman whose character claims esteem and admiration. When the offer of help was withdrawn, and she was faced by complete failure, she showed that the mental courage which made her launch her scheme was a permanent possession. After a disappointment, the keenness of which only those who have read her writings can appreciate, she continued by clear argument and "pertinent" writing to maintain that the inferiority of women to men, where it existed, was a matter not of nature but of education.

Writers as far apart in religious and social feeling as Swift and Defoe and Lady Mary Wortley Montagu noticed the haphazard upbringing of the clever women whom they met in the London drawing-rooms of their day, "the unaccountable wild method", as Steele said, "in the education of the better half of the world, the women". The problem was already half realized, and the steady pressure of Mary Astell's continuous and lucid reasoning must have had its effect.

Much as Mary Astell loved women, she did not flatter them. "Pardon me", she says, "the seeming rudeness of this Proposal, which goes upon a supposition that there is something amiss in you, which it is intended to amend" (Pt. I, p. 16).[1] She argued that the ignorance of women made them in marriage the easy victims of fortune-hunters. She saw, too, with deep pity, that the life of an unmarried gentlewoman was, in the greater number of cases, an unhappiness to herself and a burden to others. The ladies who entered her Seminary would, she hoped, receive in it a real mental training. If they married, their characters and their principles would be strong enough to support them in that state, while if they remained single, a cultivated mind and a devotion to others would make them useful and honoured. She herself sums up her purpose in founding her Seminary as no less a thing than "to stock the Kingdom with pious and prudent Ladies" (Pt. I, p. 73).

No charge of exaggerating the unhappy position of the women at the end of the seventeenth and the beginning of the eighteenth centuries was brought against Mary Astell in her own day; nor do I think that such a charge has been made since. The criticism of her contemporaries was that, in the words of Dean Atterbury, "she has not the decent manner of insinu-

[1] My references to Part I of the *Proposal* are to the first edition (1694), and those to Part II, to the edition of 1697.

ating what she means, but is now and then a little shocking in her expressions".[1]   Her admirers will admit that she hit hard, and that her language was not always more pleasing to the drawing-rooms of her own day than it would be to those of ours.

But the fact that Mary Astell was so far in advance of her time on one question did not prevent her from living in the general intellectual atmosphere of her period and her class. In her *Proposal*, and when treating of education in her other writings, she confines herself to the condition of ladies of quality; though at the end of her life, when her plan of helping the ladies of her own social world must have seemed a thing of the past, she started a school for the daughters of the pensioners in Chelsea Hospital. In *The Christian Religion as profess'd by a Daughter of the Church of England* (1705), she claims that a "Christian Woman must not be a Child in Understanding" (p. 6). But it is difficult to recognize the Mary Astell we know when she says that even if some of those whom God has appointed should lead her into error: "I am safer in my Obedience than I could have been with Truth in a disorderly way." In *A Fair Way with the Dissenters and their Patrons* (1704), she leaves us in no doubt as to her attitude towards half the English people of her time. While answering Defoe's ironical pamphlet, *The Shortest Way with the Dissenters*, she says: "I shall frankly own with an Ingenuity they would do well to Practise, that the Total Destruction of Dissenters as a

[1] *Mary Astell*, by Florence M. Smith, p. 116.

Party (the Barbarous Usage that More Short Ways is so afraid of) is indeed our design. . . . For if I do not make it out before I have done, that to strike at the Root of the Dissenting Interest, to extirpate and destroy Dissention, and hinder its succession in the Nation [by such measures as the Bill against Occasional Conformity] neither hurts the Consciences, the Persons, nor the Estates of the Dissenters, then I do nothing" (p. 3).

In her Seminary no Dissenters would have been found. Nor would there have been within its walls members of the lower orders of society; nor any one whose birth was not what she calls "generous". She accepts, as part of God's order on earth, the wealth of one social class and the poverty of the other. "For unless we have very strange Notions of the Divine Wisdom", she says, "we must needs allow that every one is placed in such a Station as they are fitted for" (Pt. II, p. 206). She suggests that even in Heaven some of these distinctions will probably be allowed to continue. For although an acceptance of the truths of the gospel is enough to ensure entrance to Heaven for the lowliest, yet ladies of quality who have had time on earth to cultivate their understandings will have higher joys than others (Pt. II, p. 207). But she deals faithfully with ladies who fail to make good use of their leisure. Of such she says: "They have nothing to do but to glorify God, and to benefit their Neighbours, and she who does not thus improve her Talent is more vile and despicable than the meanest Creature"

(Pt. I, p. 146). This is one instance of many which show that Mary Astell expressed herself with as much warmth about women who neglected their opportunities as she did about men, a point which has been missed by those who have written of her as a feminist partisan. Nor can we appreciate the force of her championship of the right of women to cultivate their minds, unless we understand that she invited the disapproval of a society whose institutions she honoured, and not, as is so often the case with pioneers, of one that she condemned and despised.

Her Seminary was to be a place of retirement for ladies of quality who, under the supervision of other ladies of quality, would have time to cultivate their minds and exercise their religion in a more serious and consistent manner than was possible in what she describes as "the cumbersome and infectious World" (Pt. I, p. 63). In Part I of the *Proposal*, she speaks of the College as a "Monastry, or if you will (to avoid giving offence to the scrupulous and injudicious, by names which tho innocent in themselves, have been abus'd by superstitious Practices) we will call it a Religious Retirement, and such as shall have a double aspect, being not only a Retreat from the World for those who desire that advantage, but likewise, an institution and previous discipline, to fit us to do the greatest good in it" (Pt. I, p. 61). And when further emphasizing the distinction between her scheme and Roman Catholicism, she says: "Piety shall not be roughly impos'd, but wisely insinuated by . . . the continual and most powerful Sermon of an holy Life. And since Inclination can't be forc'd . . . there shall be no Vows or irrevocable Obligations, not so much as the fear of Reproach to keep our Ladies here any longer than they desire. No: Ev'ry act of our Religious Votary shall be voluntary and free, and no other tye but the Pleasure, the Glory, and Advantage of this blessed Retirement to confine her to it" (Pt. I, p. 105). A great deal of time was to be given to religious observances; and for herself and her ladies religion was to include an attitude towards life and to provide them with rules of conduct. Of those who fail in the genuine Christian spirit, she says: "the mistaken person thinks the being often on her knees, attones for all the miscarriages of her Conversation"; and: "the true end of all our Prayers and external Observances is to work our minds into a truly Christian temper, to obtain for us the Empire of our Passions" (Pt. I, pp. 57, 58). Her ladies were to go back to the world so strengthened in mind that they could estimate at their true value "the Fustian Complements" and "Fulsome Flatteries" of their admirers (Pt. I, p. 5).

She hoped to end the pathos of purely mercenary marriages or despised and idle spinsterhood. In retirement, her ladies would have that which they lacked most, and still lack—leisure. Mary Astell speaks of the waste of women's time in words with which all women will sympathize. "So unreasonable is the humour of the World, that those who would reckon it a rudeness to make so bold with our Mony, never scruple to waste and rob us of this infinitely more precious Treasure" (Pt. I, p. 120). "Here will be no impertinent Visits. No foolish Amours." "In Dressing, that grand Devourer, and its concomitants, very little time will be spent . . . so that here's a huge treasure gain'd" (Pt. I, pp. 106–107).

The story that she refused herself to callers, when at home in her house at Chelsea, has been regarded as a legend, rather, I fancy, on the ground that such a step was too bold even for Mary Astell than on any evidence against its being true. But leisure was for her only a means to an end. Again and again she says that mental training is the only defence for a woman against the fraud and shameless bargaining of so many marriages. "She will not here be inveigled and impos'd on, will neither be bought nor sold" (Pt. I, p. 146). "It is", she writes in her *Reflections on Marriage*, "the hardest thing in the World for a Woman to know that a Man is not Mercenary" (p. 38). Lady Mary Wortley Montagu, in a letter to her future husband, writes: "People in my way are sold like Slaves; and I cannot tell what price my masters will put on me." Steele, for whom Mary Astell had little respect or sympathy, says that if the system of marriage settlements could be reformed, "a fine woman would no more be set up to auction as she is now".

In Mary Astell's Seminary, "she who has more mony than Discretion, need not curse her Stars, for being expos'd a prey to bold importunate and rapacious Vultures" (Pt. I, p. 146). This description of some of

the young men of the best families of her time may
not have commended itself to their friends. But it was
in the interests of young men, as well as young women,
that a protest against marriage by purchase should be
made. Parental authority, in the case of boys as well
as girls, was severe to a point that is unknown in our
time; and many a young man who could not accu-
rately have been described as a "rapacious Vulture",
must have made, from fear and a mistaken sense of
duty, a purely mercenary marriage.

Mary Astell was prepared to help another class of
gentlewoman, who had nothing to fear from rapacious
suitors, "the Daughters of Gentlemen who have fallen
into decay". Such ladies had little chance of making
what she would have considered suitable marriages,
on account of the large dowries required by parents
in their own station of life. They, she says, would "be
preserved from great Dishonours, and put in a comfortable way of subsisting, being either received into
the House, if they incline to it, or otherwise dispos'd
of" (Pt. I, p. 149).

She accepted marriage as a divinely appointed
state of subjection for women. A lady of quality
should not fall in love. Modesty required "that a
Woman should not love before Marriage, but only
make choice of one whom she can love hereafter: She
who has none but innocent affections being easily able
to fix them where Duty requires" (Pt. I, p. 147).
Nor should a lady marry outside her class. If a
suitor inferior in money or social position offers her

marriage, the presumption, nearly always present in a man's proposals, that he is seeking her money is, in this case, a practical certainty. But more than this, Mary Astell urges that if a lady had been placed by God in a position above petty cares, with leisure to prepare for Heaven, she has no right by marrying a poor man to become a "household drudge". Such conduct she describes as "ill-manners to Heaven". She did not, however, accept this position without a mental struggle. Though marriage was divinely appointed, it was not, in her view, appointed with any idea of the happiness of women. It was an institution which gave them unique opportunities of exercising the qualities of patience and endurance, and therefore an excellent preparation for Heaven. Her appeal to women in her book is to exercise these virtues, and to men not to be guilty of the meanness of taking advantage of their position to inflict unnecessary humiliation and suffering.

She only claimed for the ladies in her Seminary the right to remain single and to refuse unsuitable marriages. If friends had provided a Christian and ingenuous gentleman, equal in all ways to the lady whom he addressed, she assumes that he would be accepted. More than this, to fathers of small means she offers, as one of the inducements to place daughters in her Seminary, that in spite of the absence of dowry, they may have opportunities of marriage. In explaining the expression "or otherwise dispos'd of" she says, quite plainly, that virtuous and prudent gentlemen might apply to her Seminary for wives. "Such a Lady," she tells them, "if she bring less will not waste so much", and the gentlemen who have chosen them, as they are all ladies of quality, will have the satisfaction of "preserving the purity of their blood", rather than gaining "a weighty bag" with a "wealthy upstart" (Pt. I, pp. 158–159).

One practical point of great importance, on which Mary Astell always insists when she speaks of marriage in connection with her educational scheme, is that ladies of her Seminary will have received such a mental training as will enable them to teach their own children. In marriage she says: "Education of Children is a most necessary Employment, perhaps the chief of those who have any." Again she says: "The Foundation of Education on which in a great measure the success of all depends, shou'd be laid by the Mother, for Fathers find other Business, they will not be confined to such a laborious work, they have not such opportunities of observing a Child's Temper nor are the greater part of them like to do much good, since Precepts contradicted by Example seldom prove effectual" (Pt. II, p. 210).

But it is clear that many ladies of wealth who came under her influence would remain single; and that many women without dowries, in spite of their thrift and good birth, would have no choice in the matter. For spinsters, either from choice or necessity, Mary Astell has the greatest sympathy. It is not easy for the many independent and honoured single women of our day to put themselves back two hundred or even one hundred years, when the position of unmarried ladies was, indeed, in the greater number of cases most miserable. Mary Astell loved to think that in her retreat, solitude, instead of a terror, would be a delight.

Those who wished might stay on in her Seminary, honourably employed in teaching the new-comers. But whether they stayed or returned to the world, "Knowledge", she says, "will not lie dead upon their hands who have no Children to Instruct; the whole World is a single Lady's Family, her opportunities of doing good are not lessen'd but encreas'd by her being unconfin'd. Particular Obligations do not contract her mind, but her beneficence moves in the largest sphere. And perhaps the Glory of reforming this Prophane and Profligate Age is reserv'd for you Ladies" (Pt. II, p. 211).

Mary Astell only gives us rough indications of the financial and practical arrangements, which she calls "the Temporals", of her institution. She argues that five or six hundred pounds is very little for a parent to give with a daughter, when one considers the dowries expected in the world. "For this", she says, "they may honourably dispose of them without impairing their Estates. Five or six hundred pounds, may be easily spar'd with a Daughter, when so many thousands would go deep: and yet as the world goes be a very inconsiderable Fortune for Ladies of their Birth" (Pt. I, p. 158). If, she argues, ladies should reach a mature age unmarried, it is thrift on the part of parents to provide for them in this way, for worse things may happen. "The poor Lady, having past the prime of her years in Gaity and Company, in running the Circle of all the Vanities of the Town, having spread all her Nets and used all her arts for conquest, and finding that the Bait fails where she would have it take, and having all this while been so overcareful of her Body, that she has had no time to improve her Mind, which therefore affords her no safe retreat now she meets with Disappointments abroad, and growing every day more and more sensible that the respect which us'd to be paid to her decays as fast as her Beauty, quite terrified with the dreadful name of *Old Maid*, which yet none but fools will reproach her with, nor any wise woman be afraid of . . . she flies to some dishonourable Match, as her last tho' much mistaken Refuge." What father would not spare some thousands to prevent a match which ends in his finding himself with "an idle Fellow and perhaps a race of beggarly Children to hang on him and provide for?" (Pt. I, pp. 160–161).

When she deals with the feeding and clothing of her College, Mary Astell's faith in the effect on the mind of the contemplation of truth has a childlike quality of trustfulness. "As to Lodging, Habit and Diet," she says, "they may be quickly resolv'd on by the Ladies who shall subscribe; who I doubt not will make choice of what is most plain and decent, what Nature, not Luxury, requires" (Pt. I, p. 94). Among her "Religious", content will reign; for she is convinced that: "She who truly loves her self will never waste that Money on a decaying Carkass, which if prudently disburs'd, would procure her an eternal Mansion" (Pt. I, p. 96).

But, after all, Mary Astell's chief claim to be a pioneer in the history of the emancipation of women is educational. On this side she always emphasizes the training of the mind rather than the mere acquisition of knowledge. She herself was a student of Locke and Descartes. Philosophy was, she believed, a subject specially suitable for women. "Since it is allow'd on all hands that the Mens Business is without Doors, and that theirs is an Active Life; Women who ought to be Retir'd, are for this reason design'd by Providence for Speculation. . . . And I make no question but great Improvments might be made in the Sciences, were not Women Enviously excluded from this their proper Business."[1] French, she says, is understood by most of them, and adds that, since this is so, "methinks they may much better improve it by the study of Philosophy (as I hear the French Ladies do), Des Cartes, Malebranche and others, than by reading idle novels and Romances". And again: "Why shall it not be thought as genteel, to understand French Philosophy, as to be accoutred in a French Mode? Let therefore the famous Madam D'Acier, Scudery, &c., and our own incomparable Orinda, excite the Emulation of the English Ladies" (Pt. I, pp. 85–86). She

[1] *The Christian Religion of a Daughter of the Church of England*, p. 296.

has faith that women may reach, in their solitude, the highest regions of thought; and even that they may do original work in those regions. But "thinking is a Pain to those who have disused it". Her students are not to trouble themselves "in turning over a large number of Books, but take care to understand and digest a few well chosen ones", which "are fuller of Matter than Words, which diffuse a Light through every part of their Subject, do not skim, but Penetrate to the Bottom, and then no matter whether she be able to tell what fanciful people have said about them" (Pt. II, p. 109). Philosophy was, however, to be kept in close connection with conduct. "Truths merely speculative and which have no influence upon Practice, which neither contribute to the good of Soul or Body, are but idle Amusements, and impertinent and criminal waste of Time" (Pt. II, p. 64).

Next to philosophy she attached most importance to the study of the English language. "The Men may have unrivall'd the Glory of speaking as many Languages as Babel afforded, we only desire to express ourselves Pertinently in One." "Obscurity, one of the greatest faults in Writing, does commonly proceed from a want of Meditation" (Pt. II, p. 177). Even an honest writer may "fall in to it by reason that his ideas being become familiar to himself by frequent Meditation", he does not realize that they may be obscure to the reader. Or again: "We shou'd fold up our Thoughts so closely and neatly, expressing them in such significant tho few words as that the Readers

Mind may easily open and enlarge them. . . ." "By putting every thing in its proper place with due Order and Connexion, the Readers Mind is gently led where the Writer wou'd have it. Such a Stile is Easy without Softness, Copious as that signifies the omission of nothing necessary, yet not Wordy and Tedious; nor stuft with Nauseous Repititions" (Pt. II, pp. 178–179). Women are "generally accused of writing false English", but this she does not think is as common as is supposed. "What they most commonly fail in is the Particles and Connexion, and that generally thro' a Briskness of Temper which makes them forget, or Hast that will not suffer 'em to read over again what went before" (Pt. II, p. 193).

Advanced and enlightened as Mary Astell was on the teaching of English, she was not altogether sure that her ladies would attain to correct spelling. She gives this rather strange advice on the way to learn to spell. "And as to Spelling which they are said to be defective in, if they don't believe as they are usually told, that its fit for 'em to be so, and that to write exactly is too Pedantic, they may soon correct that fault, by pronouncing their words aright and Spelling 'em accordingly." If her ladies should, however, fail in this matter, she adds, "the fault will be very Venial and Custom rather to blame than we" (Pt. II, pp. 192–193).

She never claimed for women entrance into the professions; she leaves all honourable and remunerative employments in the hands of men. Speaking, for instance, of the teaching of oratory: "As for Pronunciation, though it takes more with some Auditors many times than Good Sense, there need be little said of it here, since Women have no business with the Pulpit, the Bar or St. Stephens Chapel" (Pt. II, p. 192). As for the men: "They may busy their Heads with Affairs of State . . . our only endeavour shall be to be absolute Monarchs of our own Bosoms. They shall still if they please dispute about Religion, let 'em only give us leave to Understand and Practice it."

It is clear that Mary Astell's friends hoped that she would have undertaken the management of the College. But she argues that the ladies who took charge of "our Religious" would need "a more exact Knowledge of Human Nature, a greater Experience of the World, and of those differences which arise from Constitution, Age, Education, receiv'd Opinions, than I can pretend to". She had looked for joint control by those "who have had so much Divinity in their Minds to design such a noble work" (Pt. II, p. 278).

But if Queen Anne had not withdrawn her offer of ten thousand pounds, and the Seminary had been started, its success would only have been possible if it had had at its head a woman with Mary Astell's unusual gifts. Under her direction, such an experiment must have left an honourable record in the history of women's education; although her College might not have been, as she hoped, "a type and antipast of Heaven" (Pt. I, p. 71). Her high ideal and her power of patient work were just what were needed in

any one who undertook so difficult a task. And more
than this, her sympathy with the lives of women was
broader than her social theories lead one to expect.
We never hear of her losing a friend except by death.
It is touching to find in her correspondence with Mr.
John Norris, on "Divine Love", her fear lest the
exclusive love of God, in which he believed, should be
inconsistent with her love of her fellow-women. "I
am loath", she writes, "to abandon all thoughts of
Friendship both because it is one of the brightest
vertues and because I have the noblest Designs in it.
Fain would I rescue my Sex or at least as many of
them as come within my little sphere from that Meanness of Spirit into which the Generality of them are
sunk." And of friendship she says it "makes no distinction betwixt its Friend and its self, except that in
Temporals it prefers her interest".

Among her friends were the Lady Elizabeth
Hastings whom Steele made famous, and Lady Mary
Wortley Montagu. It is more surprising that she wrote
with tolerance and good feeling of her Chelsea neigh-
bour, the Duchess of Mazarin. The Duchess's published *Memoirs*, which Mary Astell had read, made
any illusion as to the prudence of her past conduct
impossible; but she only regrets the waste of a vigorous
mind and brave character, and that "she who was
capable of being a great Ornament to her Family and
Blessing to the Age she liv'd in, should only serve
(to say no worse) as an unhappy Shipwrack to point
out the dangers of an ill-Education and unequal

Marriage". "Had Madam Mazarine's Education," she says, "made a right improvement of her Wit and Sense, we should not have found her seeking Relief by such imprudent, not to say Scandalous Methods, as the running away in Disguise with a Spruce Cavalier" (*Reflections upon Marriage*, pp. 4, 5).

But Mary Astell's fame does not rest only on the fact that she once made a proposal which, if it had been adopted, would have done great good. Her writings have force and originality. Few men or women could have read them in her lifetime, or can read them now, without being influenced in action and moved at heart by her plea. To women she appeals to get out of "the woful incogitancy we have slipt in to, awaken our sleeping Powers, and make use of the Reason, which God has given us". Women, she insists, "need not take up with mean things, since (if they are not wanting to themselves) they are capable of the best". "There is no reason they should be content to be Cyphers in the World, useless at the best, and in a little time a burden and nuisance to all about them" (Pt. I, p. 24). Many a woman, through her writing, must have seen for the first time how much was wrong within as well as without in her life. The condition Society has imposed on us, she says, "shortens our Views, contracts our Minds, exposes to a thousand practical Errors and renders Improvment impossible".

At the Jubilee of Newnham College, Cambridge, in July 1921, I thought of Mary Astell. I wondered

I

what, if she had been there, she would have said of the women I saw around me. At one moment I felt how great her joy would have been that so many of her hopes were fulfilled. At the next I was conscious that she would have received shocks. There among us, on equal terms, were daughters of the Church of England and those of whom she speaks "as the dearest Spawn of the Church of Rome, our English Dissenters". She would have recognized as ladies of quality only a minority, and she would have seen in authority ladies whom she would have described as "mercenaries" (Pt. I, p. 148), who receive salaries for their work and are proud to do so; she would have learnt that they are honoured by their College and by a wider world, as no amateur can be in our modern life. But the real descendants of this gallant single lady, who, with some notable exceptions, had the whole world for her family, are not those who think now as she thought two hundred years ago, but those who with trained minds have set out to examine and to remedy the evils of their own time. In our days, as in hers, there is in Mary Astell's words, "A Sort of Bravery of the Mind and Soul".

ELIZABETH ELSTOB

CHAPTER V

ELIZABETH ELSTOB

ELIZABETH ELSTOB (1683–1756) was one of the most learned students of Anglo-Saxon and the early Teutonic languages of her time in England; and her life poignantly illustrates the difficulties which a woman scholar, however gifted and however industrious, had then to face.

She was the daughter of Ralph Elstob, a merchant of Newcastle, and his wife Jane. She was proud of her stock, and worked with interest at her family tree. George Ballard, in a note on the *Life of William Elstob* which Elizabeth sent to him, tells us that their pedigree was in the Earl of Oxford's inestimable library, curiously drawn upon vellum with Mrs. Elstob's own hand, and that they were "on the maternal side descended from the old Kings or Princes of Wales". Her father died when Elizabeth was five years old, and all that he did and all that he said died with him. But of her mother we know one important fact: Jane Elstob was an admirer of learning, "especially in her own sex", and when she died Elizabeth, at eight years old, had already some knowledge of Latin; she knew, she tells us, her "Accidence and Grammar".[1]

She and her brother William, who at the time of their mother's death was a young man of eighteen,

[1] Ballard MSS., XLIII, 59 (in the Bodleian Library), and an article on Elizabeth Elstob by Margaret Ashdown (*Modern Language Review*, April 1925).

were left under the guardianship of her father's brother, the Rev. Charles Elstob, Prebendary of Canterbury. William, as a promising young scholar, spent five years at Eton, and opportunities were afterwards found for him at Cambridge and Oxford. But all we know of Elizabeth's life at this period is that she lived with Charles Elstob and his wife Martha for a period which she herself describes as "the space of a few years",[1] either in Canterbury or at her Uncle's living at Tillington in Sussex. She was not unhappy with them; for in 1708, when she dedicates her translation of Mlle. de Scudéry's *Essay on Glory* to her aunt, she says in the preface that: "Living in your family and under your care . . . I must always look upon as one of the most providential Blessings I have experienc'd in my whole Life. Since if anything cou'd alleviate the loss of one of the best of Mothers, you seem always to have endeavour'd the doing of it, by a succession of equal tenderness and kindness. But that which gives you a more particular Claim to this Performance, is that it is taken out of the French, in which language the Foundation of that little knowledge I have arriv'd to, was first laid in your House."

In the short autobiography which she afterwards sent to her friend George Ballard, we find that permission to learn French was only obtained with great difficulty. Whatever help her aunt may have been inclined to give, her uncle and guardian was "no friend to Women's Learning, so that she was not

[1] Ballard MSS., XLIII, 59.

suffered to proceed, notwithstanding her repeated requests that she might, being always put off with that common vulgar saying that one tongue is enough for a Woman".[1] The Rev. Charles Elstob was only expressing the received opinion of his time; and with that "common vulgar saying" he would have gone out of the story, if it had not happened that twenty-two years later Elizabeth, who in the meantime had acquired eight languages besides her own, dedicated a pamphlet to him, *Some Testimonies of Learned Men in Favour of the Intended Edition of the Saxon Homilies.*

In her uncle's house French was the only language she was allowed to learn, for in her second dedication of the *Essay on Glory* to Mrs. Randolph, a friend of her youth, she speaks of "the many happy Hours I spent with you, in which we used to sigh out our wishes to each other for a liberty to partake of the Greek and Latin stores". Elizabeth Elstob's own words show how persistent she was as a child. She tells Ballard that "Discouragement" (and we must remember that she is writing of the time when she was eight years old) "did not prevent her earnest endeavour to improve her mind; in the best manner she was able. Not only because she had a natural inclination for Books herself, but in obedience to her excellent Mother's desire."[2] We know that her later relations with her uncle were not unfriendly, for his name appears among the subscribers to her *Homily on St. Gregory's Birthday*; and after its publication in 1709 she

---

[1] Ballard MSS., XLIII, 59.   [2] Ibid., XLIII, 59.

writes, in the preface to her *English-Saxon Grammar*, that she was "engaged by the importunity of my Friends, to make a Visit to Canterbury, as well to enjoy the Conversation of my Friends and Relations there, as for that Benefit, which I hoped to receive from Change of air and freer Breathing".

William Elstob was elected a Fellow of Queen's College, Oxford, in June 1696, and six years later, when Elizabeth was nineteen years of age, he moved to London as incumbent of the united parishes of St. Swithin's and St. Mary Bothaw's. We do not know whether William and Elizabeth kept house together during any part of the years which William spent in Oxford; but she went with him to Bush Lane, near London Stone, in 1702, and stayed with him until his death from consumption in 1715. From the time that she joined her brother, her troubles in the acquisition of learning were over; for she tells us that he "very joyfully and readily assisted and encourag'd her in her Studies", and with him, she says, "she labour'd very hard as long as he liv'd".[1]

It was during these thirteen years in London, with her brother's "joyful help", that Elizabeth did the work that won for her a reputation for exact scholarship. Besides her translation of Mlle. de Scudéry's *Essay on Glory* in 1708, she published in 1709 her translation of *An English-Saxon Homily on the Birthday of St. Gregory*, and in 1713 her little pamphlet, *Some Testimonies of Learned Men in Favour of the Intended Edition*

[1] Ballard MSS., XLIII, 59.

THE
ENGLISH-SAXON
GRAMMAR.

RAMMAR is the Art of Speaking and Writing, truly and properly. In Speaking we use certain Signs, which are necessary to discover our Thoughts to one another. These Signs, are Sound, and Voice.

But besides, Sound, and Voice, by which we are able to converse with one another when present; There are other Signs have been invented, where these Sounds cannot be heard, to supply the want of them in such manner, as that we may both converse with one another at a distance, and communicate our Thoughts to future Ages.

The first of these Signs belongs properly to Speech, or unwritten Discourse. The latter are made use of in Writing.

Hence the *Greeks*, from whom we receiv'd the first Rudiments of this Art, have deliver'd down to us the Names

FIRST PAGE OF "THE RUDIMENTS OF GRAMMAR FOR THE ENGLISH-SAXON TONGUE", BY ELIZABETH ELSTOB

of the Saxon Homilies. In 1715 her modest *English-Saxon Grammar* came out. She undertook it, she says, owing to the encouragement she met with "from the ladies", on her visit to Canterbury, after the publication of her first attempt in Saxon (the *Homily on St. Gregory's Birthday*), and especially owing to the request of one young lady, "whose ingenuity and Love of Learning is well known and esteemed".

Swift, whose fame was then at its height, had written, in 1712, *A Proposal for Correcting and Improving and Ascertaining the English Tongue.* His chief complaint was against the "barbarous custom of abbreviating words". This, he says, had been "frequently done so very injudiciously that none but a Northern Ear could endure" (p. 21). By his treatment of her loved Northern tongues, and by the contempt expressed in the same pamphlet for her friend Dean Hickes's *Thesaurus,* Elizabeth was roused, and, as she tells us in her preface to the *Grammar,* "led into a Stile not so agreeable to the mildness of her sex", as she could have wished to maintain. She speaks of her opponents as "Pedagogues who huff and swagger in the height of their Arrogance". Swift, by admitting ignorance of the languages which he criticized, gave Elizabeth her opportunity. "I can speak", she says, "for the Saxon, Gothick, and Francick, or old Teutonic. . . . I never could find myself shocked with the Harshness of those Languages, which grates so much in the Ears of those that never heard them." As far as we know, Swift never answered her; but the "Saxon Lady" had made an impression. Ballard, writing to Ames twenty-three years later, on June 29, 1737, says: "Indeed I thought that the bad success Dean Swift had met with in this affair from the incomparably learned and ingenious Mrs. Elstob, would have deterred all others from once opening their mouths in this affair."[1] As late as 1839, when, owing to a revival of interest in Anglo-Saxon, the *Homily on St. Gregory's Birthday* was reprinted (being chosen on account of the accuracy of the text), the writer of the preface, speaking of Elizabeth, rather curiously assumes that no one without an independent income would have dared write as she did. "How far Mrs. Elstob was easy or otherwise, in point of fortune, after her brother's death, does not appear, though from the tone and manner of the preface to her English-Saxon Grammar it may perhaps be inferred that at the time of that publication she was not under pecuniary difficulties."[2] Elizabeth had proved that she could defend her friends, and that her learning, acknowledged by the small group of Saxon scholars, made her formidable in a larger world.

The author of the *Thesaurus*, Dean Hickes (as he is persistently called, although as a non-juror he was deprived of the deanery of Worcester), was one of the most devoted friends of Elizabeth and her brother. In 1713, in the dedication of his *Sermons on Several Subjects* to Dr. John Montagu, he speaks of Mrs.

---

[1] Nichols's *Illustrations of Literary History* (1822), Chap. IV, p. 212.
[2] Preface, by J. S. C., to reprint of the *Homily on St. Gregory's Birthday* (1839).

Elstob's "incredible industry", and of her "learned and useful notes". Cambridge University entrusted at least one valuable manuscript to her, for Ralph Thoresby, in his *Diary* of July 8, 1712, says that he has been at Parson Elstob's, and that Elizabeth, whom he calls the "Saxon Nymph", showed "me a large Volume of Saxon Homilies from the public library at Cambridge, being an antient and Noble manuscript upon parchment, which she is now transcribing in a curious character for the press, with her translation from the Latin and the Saxon".

Her translation of the *Homily on the Birthday of St. Gregory* had been printed by W. Bowyer, whose house and types were destroyed by fire in 1713. Lord Chief Justice Parker (afterwards Lord Macclesfield) asked her to draw the originals of a new Saxon type, from which Bowyer printed her *English-Saxon Grammar*. After Bowyer's death the punches and matrices of this type were presented by his son to the University of Oxford.[1] She tells Ballard, on December 4, 1736, of this incident. "I did it", she writes, "from the best I could meet with, yet I am not a little proud that it was approv'd on."[2]

The life in Bush Lane during these years cannot have been an easy one. William worked hard, both as a scholar and as incumbent, and Elizabeth probably helped him in his parish as well as in the house. But

---

[1] *Anecdotes Biographical and Literary of the late Mr. W. Bowyer, printer* (1778).

[2] Ballard MSS., XLIII, 59.

they had genuine pleasures. They were visited by
some of the men who were beginning to be called
"antiquaries", and who founded the Society of Antiquaries, of which William, who joined in 1708, was
one of the early members.[1] Among these men some
were perhaps mere collectors, and were laughed
at just as the early naturalists were laughed at by
Addison when he speaks of men who "utter Strangers
to common Occurrences of Life . . . scarce know a
Horse from an Ox, but were able to discover the Sex
of a Cockle, or describe the generation of a Mite, in
all its circumstances".[2] And yet, just as the naturalists
were preparing the way for modern biology, the antiquaries, while collecting coins and faithfully copying
inscriptions, were helping to provide material for a
science of history in which Elizabeth's exact tran-
scriptions and translations of the surviving Anglo-
Saxon documents were of real importance.

Between the brother and sister there was the rare
affection which comes when kinship is combined with
common intellectual interests. That William found in
her something more than a housekeeper, or even than
a much-loved pupil, we know from the Latin preface
which he wrote to his translation into Latin of the
Anglo-Saxon *Homily on St. Gregory's Birthday*, which
Elizabeth had translated into English (1709). Here,
after references to her modesty, he speaks of her as
"the dear and tireless companion of my studies". He

---

[1] Nichols's *Literary Anecdotes*, Vol. VI, p. 143.
[2] *Tatler*, 216.

was writing at this time his *Essay on the Great Affinity of the two Professions of Divinity and Law*, in which he defended the Clergy's "concerning themselves in Political matters", and an "*Essay on the Latin Tongue*", which, he says, he intends for those "adult persons . . . who have been either neglected or been frightened from receiving the benefit of that kind of education in their infancy". He also nearly finished what would have been, if he had lived longer, his most important work, an edition of the Saxon Laws, with a prefatory history of the origin and progress of the English Laws down to the Conquest.

This time of comparative happiness and vigorous intellectual activity for both Elizabeth and William Elstob was short. William Elstob was consumptive, and the combination of ill-paid City parochial work with close study was the worst possible for his case. At the very end of his life, he and his friends made efforts to get him removed to a more suitable living. In 1712, when William had been ten years in the City, we have a letter of his to Wanley, expressing a hope that the Lord Treasurer would think him the proper person to fill a vacancy at Canterbury. He mentions he has been ten years in London, and says, "our City livings are small in revenue and our expenses great in comparison".[1] He had "neither the strength, nor the necessary assurance requisite for a man to improve his fortune by popular preaching".

[1] We are told by Nichols that his joint parishes were at this time worth £140 a year. Nichols's *Literary Anecdotes*, Vol. IV, p. 114.

But the main attraction for him at Canterbury is the library. He thinks that if "my Lord Treasurer were made acquainted that the library there had a good many books in the Canon, Civil and Common Law as he judged proper in the Work I have engaged in", he might think him the proper person to fill the vacancy. Harley, the Lord Treasurer (the collector of the Harley Manuscripts in the British Museum), was himself an antiquary, and Dean Hickes writes to him of William's suitability for this post; he says that he is a man "whose modesty hath made him an obscure person, and ever will make him so, unless some kind patron of good learning will bring him into light". Hickes expects, however, that "my Lord Keeper hath a domestic chaplain of his own to whom he will think fit to give the preferment mentioned in the enclosed". Apparently this was the case, for William Elstob stayed on in Bush Lane. In 1713 there was a vacancy at Lincoln's Inn, and this time William himself solicits Lord Chief Justice Parker for his interest on his behalf. He says in his letter that he had been "a preacher in the City eleven years, and diligent in his profession, as well as laborious in other matters, without seeking or finding such assistances as are both useful and necessary to such as converse with books".

To both William and Elizabeth Elstob, "converse with books" was their very life, but to neither of them was ever given full opportunity for this converse. Again William was unsuccessful in his appeal, and the end of his life is best described by Ballard in the preface which he wrote in 1751 to King Alfred's translation of Orosius's *History of the World*. "Between", Ballard says (p. 27), "the discharge of the Duty of his Office and his unwearied application to the Oriental as well as the Septentrional Languages, and by his Writing, Publishing, and carrying on many other learned and laborious Works with too great intentness, he impaired and weakened his too tender constitution, which was soon followed by a long indisposition. This indisposition rendered him unfit for much attention . . . so that he was prevented by death in this and other great designs for the Publick good."

William Elstob died not much more than a year after his application to be moved to Lincoln's Inn, and he was buried in the chancel of the Church of St. Swithin's, in the parish which he had so eagerly longed to leave. In the formal but transparently sincere life of her brother, which Elizabeth copied in her beautiful handwriting and sent to Ballard in January 1736, she pays tribute to William's scholarship, to his "piety and patriotism", the "universality of his genius", and "the sweetness of his temper".[1] But in a spontaneous note, warmed by some practical evidence of Ballard's genuine friendship, she gives us insight into a lovable character. She can think of nothing, she says, writing on March 12, 1737, "that can Illustrate my dear Brother's character more than by comparing him to your Good Self, in his generosity

[1] Ballard MSS., XLIII, 14.

and Fidelity to his Friend, he never thinking himself more truly happy than when he had it in his power to serve his Friend, without giving him the trouble to ask him".[1]

It is probable that while Elizabeth nursed her dying brother, her own future was little in her thoughts, and that, with the sympathetic appreciation which she had met with for her learning, she had no clear idea of what it would mean to be left alone in the world, a scholar, when that scholar was a woman.

When her brother died in 1715, Elizabeth was thirty-one, young in years for a scholar. The idea persists that Elizabeth at that time had private means. Mrs. Chapone, in Nichols's account of her appeal to Queen Caroline, speaks of Elizabeth's "affluence during her brother's lifetime".[2] Mr. Rowe Mores, who at the end of his life wrote *A Dissertation upon English Typographical Founders and Founderies* (1779), speaks of Elizabeth as "a Northern Lady of an antient family and a genteel fortune; but", he says, "she pursued too much the drug called learning and in that pursuit failed of being careful of any one thing necessary".[3] But there is a suspicious vagueness about both these statements, and it is quite possible that if the Elstobs ever had any private fortune, it was during these thirteen years gradually absorbed in household expenses and the administration of two poor City

[1] Ballard MSS., XLIII, 36.
[2] Nichols's *Literary Anecdotes*, Vol. VI, p. 311.
[3] Ibid., Vol. IV, p. 130.

parishes, particularly as in her life of her brother, Elizabeth says that he was "generous to all, which was his greatest fault".[1] It is notable that this is the only word of criticism in any of her references to him.

One fact is certain; at William's death Elizabeth found herself destitute, encumbered with debts, and, for the first time in her life, faced with the problem of earning her living. What could she do? Though William's hopes as a scholar had been disappointed, yet the patronage of the Church had given him security against destitution. The fact that all support for scholarship was in the hands of the Church was criticized, even at the time, on the ground that it excluded Dissenters of every kind from benefiting by it. It has not, perhaps, been noticed that after the suppression of the nunneries, women scholars were as completely excluded as Dissenters from any share in the revenues of the Church of England. If Elizabeth Elstob had lived to-day, she might have filled a post in a college, or in a girls' school where advanced work was being done; but in 1715 there were no such schools or colleges. She had completed, and had on her hands, the translation of *Ælfric's Sermons*, a scholarly work to which she had given the best years of her life. But there were then few opportunities for the publication of learned books outside the fields of Anglican theology and classical culture. The resources of the Oxford and Cambridge University presses were limited. The one method that made it possible

[1] Ballard MSS., XLIII, 14.

K

to produce such a work was publication by subscription.

If the material for a history of publication by subscription could be obtained, it would show that that
system involved more possibilities of disappointment
and humiliation for the author and the bookseller
than any system devised before or since. The arrangements varied in individual cases. Major Putnam, for
instance, states that the money from the subscribers
was not generally forthcoming until the bookseller
actually sent the book. But apparently, as in the case
of Dr. Johnson's *Shakespeare*, money was often advanced, through or by the bookseller, on which the
author lived while he wrote the expected book. In
some cases friends handed their subscriptions to the
author directly, as Ralph Thoresby seems to have
done. On July 4, 1714, he says: "Mr. Elstob preached
very well. . . . I dined with the learned author and
his ingenious sister, who besides the Saxon Homily (to
which I have subscribed) has in the press also a Saxon
Grammar."[1]

Hearne's *Diary* and the Ballard Manuscripts show
that Elizabeth had been personally occupied, before
her brother's death, in getting subscriptions for her
translation of *Ælfric's Sermons*. As early as December
1712, Dean Hickes was writing enthusiastically about
this work to Dr. Charlett, Master of University
College, Oxford. Mrs. Elstob, he says, had brought it
"to be printed at your presse. . . ." "The publication

[1] *Diary of Ralph Thoresby*, II, p. 229.

of the Manuscript she hath brought (the most correct I ever saw or read) will be of great advantage against the Papists." He also says that Mrs. Elstob will be counted abroad "as great an ornament in her way as Madame D'Acier is to France. . . . Were I at Oxford, I should be a great Sollicitor for her. . . ."[1] Nichols quotes a letter from Elizabeth in 1714, thanking Lord Oxford for having obtained for her the Royal Bounty towards printing the *Saxon Homilies*.[2] W. Bishop of Gray's Inn, in 1717, writing to Dr. Charlett, says: "Being this day with Mrs. Elstob I find by her that she has great encouragement and many subscribers at Cambridge, and little countenance and few subscribers in Oxford"; and he expresses great surprise that this should be so, "not doubting but the Colleges would all subscribe for their libraries".[3]

While all these subscriptions were coming in, Elizabeth was nursing her dying brother. When he died, it is natural that she should have still clung tenaciously to the idea of bringing out her book. Not only was it her most important work, but she must have felt her honour involved with her subscribers, whether they were her personal friends or professional booksellers. Her own *Grammar*, and what of William's work had been printed, had been published in this way, and it is little wonder that she had hoped that the knowledge which from girlhood she had acquired with what Dean Hickes called "incredible industry" might both

[1] Ballard MSS., XII, 129.
[2] Nichols's *Literary Anecdotes*, Vol. IV, p. 127.
[3] Ballard MSS., XXXII, 19.

be of use in the world and provide her with an honourable means of livelihood.

We can infer the growth and slow death of that hope from scattered references in Hearne's diaries. A reference to the Elstobs in October 1709 is noticeably unfriendly. He writes of the beautiful little book (now in the British Museum) that contains Elizabeth's translation into English and William's Latin of the *Sermon on St. Gregory's Birthday*, and says: "which book, tho' it bear the name of Mrs. Elstob is chiefly owing to her brother. This small book is design'd to promote and advance Saxon knowledge; but I am much mistaken if it will not have quite a different effect and make it look mean and little." And among the "Odd Flights of Vanity",[1] he includes the "Bedrol" of subscribers, and the beautiful and restrained Latin letter to his sister from which I have quoted. But Elizabeth's proposed translation of *Ælfric's Sermons* attracted wider attention, and Hearne's tone changes. Four years later, in February 1713, he receives a letter from Mr. Bedford, who gives a message from the Dean of Worcester. "I am to desire you from him to give all the assistance and encouragement ye can to Mrs. Elstob's work." In March of the same year Hearne fears if "she meets with no better Encouragement here than I have done as yet, it will not be great".[2] In May 1715, three months after William Elstob's death, Dean Hickes writes to Hearne, "Will send a copy of

[1] *Remarks and Collections of Thos. Hearne* (Oxford Historical Society), Vol. II, p. 289.
[2] Ibid., Vol. IV, p. 93.

Mrs. Elstob's book when published".[1] In July of the same year Hearne writes to Dean Hickes, thanking him for the valuable present of Hickes's own *Thesaurus* and Mrs. Elstob's *Saxon Grammar*. "Hearty thanks," he says, quite won over to the idea that Elizabeth must be taken seriously, "Mrs. Elstob's preface is judicious, learned and elegant. Glad of the remarks on the author of the Proposals [Swift], and even more on her other opponent" [Dr. Felkin],[2] "a man", Hearne says, that had always been looked on "as a vain flashy person".[3]

In his first appeal Dean Hickes wrote by another hand, as he was too ill to write himself, and before the end of the same year, 1715, in which her brother died, Dean Hickes, the friend who had given them persistent help and admiring appreciation, died also. Hearne had, of course, innumerable other interests, and his references to Elizabeth Elstob are intermittent and casual. Sir P. Sydenham, writing to him in July 1716, says, "Much concerned that Mrs. Elstob's *Homilies of Ælfric* is not yet published". "Sorry", he adds (the news apparently is fresh to him), "for the death of her learned brother."[4] By November 1716 things were looking very black. On the 15th the Rev. T. Baker, in a letter to Humphries, says: "I am sorry I am disabled from doing you so much service as I am desirous to do, for I am so deep

[1] Hearne, Vol. V, p. 58.
[2] Dr. Felkin. His name is put in by Ballard in a letter from W. Bishop to Dr. Charlett.
[3] Hearne, Vol. V, p. 83.   [4] Ibid., Vol. V, p. 271.

with Mrs. Elstob and Mr. Strype that I have no other answer to give to my subscribers, but that I will trouble them no more till I have made good these Proposals which I doubt I shall not be able to do in haste."[1] There is a gleam of hope a fortnight later, for Hearne writes to J. Innys on November 29, 1716, that he "hears that Mrs. Elstob's book is going at last".[2] After this for two years there is silence about Elizabeth Elstob and her works.

By the autumn of 1718 it is clear that her case was desperate. Friends without doubt must have tried to help her; but the Elstobs, except to a small group, were "obscure persons". Dean Hickes had died. Bishop Smalridge is said to have given help. In the scattered and unsatisfying references to this period there is no mention of the Rev. Charles Elstob. Elizabeth may have received help from him, or she may not have appealed to him. He died in 1721. On October 16, 1718, the Rev. T. Baker, who had decided two years earlier not to trouble any further those who had subscribed through him for Elizabeth's work, writes to Mr. Humphries: "I am glad to hear Mrs. Elstob is in a condition to pay her debts, for me she may be very easy."

This effort of Elizabeth's to pay her debts was a very unsuccessful one, for a note is added in Wanley's handwriting, saying, "Mrs. Elstob has only paid a few small scores".[3] The confusion in her affairs at this

---

[1] Hearne, Vol. V, p. 337.   [2] Ibid., Vol. V, p. 358.
[3] *Notes and Queries*, 1st Series, Vol. IX, p. 7. January 7, 1854.

time must have been distressing, for Baker adds: "I could wish for sake of the University (tho' I am in no way engaged having taken up my obligations) that you could recover the book, or at least could find where it is lodged, that Mr. Brook may know where to demand it. This, I presume, may be done."

The most important loan from the Cambridge Library to Elizabeth was the manuscript of *Ælfric's Homilies*, and it is a relief to know, through the courtesy of the Librarian of Cambridge University, that the manuscript of the *Homilies* is still in the Library. For the rest of her life the subject of her books and papers was painful to Elizabeth. In July 1748 she writes to Ballard, who had made some inquiries about the papers, and tells him that she intrusted some of them to a female friend, who went abroad and was heard of no more. "It is", she says, "at least thirty years since this happen'd to me, and you may reasonably think it has made me very unhappy ever since, which if my friends were sensible of, I must believe they would avoid all occasions of bringing it to my remembrance."[1] It may be that of what remained she could not save much from her creditors, when they, in all probability, seized her goods.

Imprisonment for debt was then in force, and the climax of these years of fruitless effort and misery was reached in the autumn of 1718. On November 30th Baker, writing to Hearne, says: "If I hear of any Subscriptions, I will acquaint you, tho' I have been so

[1] Ballard MSS., XLIII, 72.

bit by Mrs. Elstob of late, who is lately gone off for debt, for whose Saxon Homilies I was above ten pounds deep."[1] So that before November 30, 1718, three years and eight months after William's death, Elizabeth Elstob had disappeared. She changed her name, and kept the secret of her hiding-place so successfully from her creditors that we to-day are in ignorance of it. In 1748 Elizabeth told George Ballard that it was thirty years since she first went into Worcestershire.[2] She must have gone to that county at once.

Her liability to imprisonment for debt was confined (by the Statute of Limitations, 1623) to six years; but her exile lasted longer. Mrs. Delany and her sister Mrs. Dewes knew where she had been, and something of what she was doing at some time during this period, for writing to her sister on December 12, 1738, Mrs. Delany says: "My mama is *very kind* in inviting Mrs. Elstob. I almost fancy she will not accept of it, because of having been there in a disguised way."[3] The references to these years of her life that Elizabeth makes to Ballard are few and grudging, and to those who have followed her in happier days, her reticence is proof enough of her sufferings. It is clear that she was working too hard in pre-eminently unsuitable work, almost certainly as a servant, in the house of some great family like the Granvilles, and that her health was giving way under the strain. Her prospects for the future were either to be kept alive by casual

[1] Hearne, Vol. VI, p. 255.   [2] Ballard MSS., XLIII, 72.
[3] Delany, *Autobiography*, II, p. 14.

charity—to come, perhaps, to one of the poor-houses of the day—or to starve.

It was due to the efforts of three new friends, Mrs. Delany[1] (at that time Mrs. Pendarves), Mrs. Sarah Chapone, and George Ballard, that she did not spend the remaining years of her life in obscure destitution. Mrs. Delany (*née* Granville, 1700–1788) was a niece of Lord Lansdowne. She was married at eighteen (in the unfounded hope that the marriage would be for the benefit of the family estates), to an elderly Cornishman, Mr. Alexander Pendarves, who died in 1724. Nineteen years later (1743) she married the Rev. Patrick Delany, afterwards Dean of Cloyne. She is famous for her skill in shellwork and paper-cutting, for her friendship as a young woman with Swift, for the many volumes of her letters and memoirs, and for being, in her old age, the patroness through whom Fanny Burney obtained the position of lady-in-waiting to Queen Charlotte.

Sarah Chapone (*née* Kirkman) was the mother-in-law of the more famous Hester Chapone (1728–1801), who wrote *Letters to a young lady on the Improvement of the Mind* (1773). Sarah Kirkman was a girlhood's friend of Mrs. Delany. She married a poor clergyman, who kept a school at Stanton in Gloucestershire, and brought up a large family. Mrs. Chapone had a fluent and persuasive pen, and an energy in well-doing that no parochial or family

[1] I have used throughout her name by her second marriage, by which she is best known.

cares ever exhausted. Through her friendship with a member of the Granville family, Mrs. Chapone was able to reach great people in the interests of "deserving objects".

Mrs. Delany says that her name for Sarah in their girlhood was "Sappho", and that they met for a time, by stealth, in the fields that joined their fathers' houses, because Mr. Granville disapproved of the friendship. He did not like Sarah, for he "loved gentleness and reserve in the behaviour of women", and found the manners of Miss Kirkman "too free and masculine". Mrs. Delany admitted sadly, in later years, that Sally was not "the perfect creature I thought her then".[1] Sally never did anything by halves. After her marriage in 1725, to the Rev. John Chapone, her accounts of domestic happiness weary Mrs. Delany, and there are signs of a slight strain in their friendship. "Sally", she tells her sister Anne Dewes, "is grown such a 'conjugal creature', that her letters are full of nothing but 'caro sposo' and 'the terrible and dreadful misfortune' of some short separation between them." Even the epistolary style, for which Sally was famous quite early in her life, falls off. "Her sense", Mrs. Delany complains, "is in masquerade since her being the half of a parson."[2] In December 1740 Mrs. Delany confessed to being bored by a "downright fire-side letter", containing news of the infant troubles of "Jacky, Dicky and

[1] Delany, *Autobiography*, I, p. 15.
[2] Ibid., I, p. 121.

Harry".[1] But the feelings of old friendship withstood these trials. Mrs. Delany's real affection for Sally, and her desire to promote her interests, never flag. Sally's style was only intermittently "downright fire-side", and her friend's permanent feeling was that Sally was thrown away as the wife of a poor clergyman in Gloucestershire. Stanton was a quiet place, so much so that when Anne Dewes is going to pay a visit there, Mrs. Delany decides not to buy the lutestring as her sister had commissioned her to do, because she considers that Anne will not need it "in a place where there is so little company". "Sally", she writes, "would shine in an assembly composed of Tulleys, Homers and Miltons, at Gloucester she is like a diamond set in jet, their dulness makes her brightness brighter."[2]

George Ballard (1706–1755) was a tailor and stay-maker. He lived in Campden (Gloucestershire) with his widowed mother, who practised as a midwife. From boyhood he had been a passionate collector of "antiquities", and Hearne's diaries contain many references to him, and to his journeys over the country-side in search of coins and old books. He published in 1752 his *Memoirs of Learned Ladies*, on which, and his valuable collection of manuscript letters in the Bodleian Library, his fame rests to-day. Mr. Mores speaks of him as "a mantua-maker, a person studious in English antiquities, laborious in his pursuits, a

[1] Delany, *Autobiography*, II, p. 137.
[2] Ibid., I, p. 586. Letter of January 4, 1736.

Saxonist, and after quitting external ornaments of the sex, a contemplator of their internal qualifications".[1] In 1750, towards the end of his life, he was given a clerkship at Magdalen College, Oxford. He was offered £100 a year, but would accept only £60, saying that he would find this sum enough for his needs. When he met Elizabeth Elstob in 1735, he was still in business in Campden. Mrs. Chapone had known Mrs. Ballard professionally, for writing to the son on October 17, 1737, she says: "I beg my sincere service to good Mrs. Ballard. I have recommended her to my sister Kirkman. . . . I shall never forget how much I owe to her skill and care."[2] Of the three friends it was George Ballard alone who was scholar enough to appreciate the work of the Elstobs. Nichols illustrates Ballard's enthusiasm for the Saxon language by describing how he "celebrated a festival which he held for his friends on having completed a transcript of a Saxon Dictionary . . . being not able to purchase it, and which he had improved with the addition of near a thousand words selected from his own reading".[3]

Mrs. Chapone was the first who tried to restore Elizabeth to a better position. On May 24, 1756, at the very end of Elizabeth's life, Mrs. Delany speaks of Sarah Chapone as having been "*the friend* who was the *first* occasion of her being brought out of

[1] Nichols's *Literary Anecdotes*, Vol. II, p. 466.
[2] Ballard MSS., XLIII, 128.
[3] Nichols's *Literary Anecdotes*, Vol. I, p. 466.

obscurity".[1] On January 6, 1736, Mr. Hastings, acknowledging a letter that Mrs. Chapone had written on Mrs. Elstob's behalf, speaks of its having been "truly generous and Christian of Mrs. Chapone the going in search of her".[2] Mrs. Chapone had probably been in communication with Elizabeth as early as 1728, ten years after her disappearance. For in 1735 Elizabeth writes to Ballard that she had just, "after seven years patience and endeavours for a school . . . obtain'd such a one as I desired".[3]

From the beginning, Mrs. Chapone had used all her energy in Elizabeth's cause. In the England of George II the most obvious means of helping her was to interest one of the "great people" in the country seats, or at Court, who concentrated in their hands nearly all the small and large patronage of the time, and who accepted the protection of learning and merit as one of the duties of an aristocracy. To get the ear of a member of these families was no easy task, and to interest royalty was harder still, but Mrs. Delany speaks of her friend Sally in her *Life* as having "an uncommon genius and an intrepid character";[4] and the first fact that we know of Mrs. Elstob after her disappearance is that through Mrs. Delany's influence a letter, written by Mrs. Chapone, had reached first Mr. Pointz (at that time tutor to Prince William), and, through him, Queen Caroline. "Never in her

---

[1] Delany, *Autobiography*, III, p. 431.
[2] Ballard MSS., XLIII, 21. [3] Ibid., XLIII, 3.
[4] Delany, *Autobiography*, I, p. 15.

life", said the Queen, had she read "a better". It so
touched her heart that she said Mrs. Elstob "need
never fear a necessitous old age whilst she lived".
"Sally's letter", Mrs. Delany writes to Anne Dewes
on October 15, 1730, "was the whole discourse of the
drawing-room. The Queen asked the Duke when he
should be able to write such a letter. He answered
honestly, 'Never'."[1] At first the Queen thought of
allowing Mrs. Elstob twenty pounds per annum, but
on second thoughts she said, "as she is so proper to be
the mistress of a boarding-school of young ladies of
higher rank, I will instead of an annual allowance,
send her one hundred pounds now, and repeat the
same at the end of every five years".[2]

This, as Mrs. Delany says, was "acting like a
Queen", and the bounty, which ceased in 1737 when
the Queen died, must have helped Elizabeth during
the years when she was looking for a school, and for a
short time after she had succeeded in finding one.
Sally Chapone no doubt stirred Mrs. Delany's interest
in the almost forgotten scholar; but it is clear that
Mrs. Delany's chief interest in what she called "the
Elstobian affair" was the hope that Sally's eloquent
letters would be the cause of her husband being
brought out of the obscurity of a Gloucestershire
parish. When in 1730 the letter reached Queen Caroline, Mrs. Delany writes: "I hope this may be a means
of serving our friend Sally, indeed Mr. Pointz asked

[1] Delany, *Autobiography*, I, p. 264.
[2] Nichols's *Literary Anecdotes*, Vol. IV, p. 133.

many particulars about Mr. Chapone, and I did him justice."[1] Mr. Pointz had assured Mrs. Delany he "will not rest till he sends him a scholar that may make his fortune; I gave Mrs. Chapone an account of my happy success last post".[2]

After Sally Chapone's striking success of interesting Queen Caroline in Mrs. Elstob, we know nothing more of her efforts on Elizabeth's behalf, or of Elizabeth's life for a period of about five years. We then find her settled, by her new friend's help, in a school in the High Street of Evesham. Tindal tells us in his *Evesham*, published in 1794, thirty-eight years after Elizabeth's death, that "some faint traces of her memory yet remain among the inhabitants of Evesham. . . . Her weekly stipend with each pupil was, as I am credibly informed, at first only a groat a week, and that she had so many of them that she hardly found time to eat."[3] So it is probable that her pupils were poor children and not those of the rank that Queen Caroline had judged her fit to teach.

George Ballard's shop at Campden was five miles from Elizabeth's school in the High Street at Evesham, and he preserved the letters which she wrote to him between August 1735 and October 1738. No one can read unmoved the story unfolded in them of overwork and failing health. In Elizabeth's first letter, of August 17, 1735, when a question of a new post arises, she hesitates, because, as she tells Ballard,

<hr />

[1] Delany, *Autobiography*, I, pp. 263, 264.
[2] Ibid., I, pp. 263, 264.   [3] Tindal's *Evesham*, p. 276.

she had "met with a great deal of Friendship and Generosity from the Good Ladies in this Place".[1] But in the same letter she writes: "I must acquaint you that I have no time to do anything till six at night, when I have done the Duty of the day and am then frequently so fatigu'd that I am oblig'd to lye down for an hour or two to rest myself and recover my Spirits."[2] Two of her letters to Ballard are written on "Little Fair Day"—which took place in Evesham on May 9 and September 11, 1736—because, she tells him, these days are the only holidays "allowed to my children and self".[3] In a letter of December 4, 1736, she speaks of her loneliness. "I assure you these long winter evenings to me are very Melancholy ones, for when my School is done my little ones leave me incapable of either reading, writing or thinking, for their noise is not out of my head till I fall asleep, which is often too late."[4] And yet every reference to her scholars or to children in these letters is a sympathetic one.

The letters also show that Ballard's friendship brought her, even at Evesham, some hours of real happiness. When the correspondence began, Elizabeth had never met him personally; he was, as she said, "a gentleman unknown".[5] Her first letter is an answer to one from him, in which he had evidently suggested that she should translate for Lady North-

[1] Ballard MSS., XLIII, 3.
[2] Ibid., XLIII, 5.   [3] Ibid., XLIII, 23.
[4] Ibid., XLIII, 29.   [5] Ibid., XLIII, 3.

PAGE OF AN "ANGLO-SAXON HOMILY", TRANSCRIBED BY ELIZABETH ELSTOB

ampton some "pieces" from the Anglo-Saxon. Elizabeth makes it clear how much she would like to have
accepted this offer. "Nothing in this world, you may
believe me Sir, would be a greater pleasure to me . . ."
"She is", she says, "never so highly gratified" as when
she hears, "of any of my Sex who employ themselves
in Laudable undertakings. Had your Proposal come
some time ago, I had been at Liberty to accept it."[1]
Now she has her School, but there is a sadder reason
for hesitating to accept what was, as far as I know,
the only work ever to be offered which might have
brought her back among scholars, and so given even
now some unity to her life. She speaks of the "unhappy
circumstances I have laboured under for several years,
which depriv'd me of leisure to follow those Studies,
which were my only delight and employment when I
had nothing else to do".[2] Ballard must have answered
that the work could be done at her leisure; for she
writes again twelve days later that she is ready to
serve and oblige the lady, "as far as my health and
business will permit". Books are her great difficulty.
"Antiquaries", she complains, "in these parts are so
scarce" that she cannot, unless Ballard has it himself,
even borrow Somner's *Dictionary*.[3]

This work for Lady Northampton was, I believe,
never done. But the offer was the beginning of her
friendship with George Ballard. He was a man who
had never accepted the standard of his day on the

[1] Ballard MSS., XLIII, 3.
[2] Ibid., XLIII, 3.   [3] Ibid., XLIII, 5.

subject of the education of women, and had always, through a certain simplicity and sympathy in his character, realized the obstacles that were put in the way of women acquiring or loving knowledge. For years, among his other activities, Ballard had collected information about the learned ladies of the past; so that when he, a young man of twenty-nine, met Elizabeth Elstob, a spinster of fifty-two, they had at once ground for friendship. The Elstobs were known and honoured by him through their writings, and he was stirred by Elizabeth's hard fate. To her other new friends, however sympathetic, she was in the first place a deserving object of charity, while he looked up to her as a scholar. She was amazed by the sympathy and interest shown in her by this "gentleman unknown", and in her letters to him we find again something of the gifted and high-spirited girl who in spite of opposition had learnt language after language.

Elizabeth, we know, prided herself on her "antient lineage", and Ballard evidently told her of his humble social position, and had doubts whether she would think him worthy of her friendship. She writes that: "The modest and humble account you are pleas'd to give of yourself, raises my esteem for you much higher than it was before, there being very few to be found who will undervalue themselves."[1] She even feels that a man of such delicacy of feeling must have a gentle pedigree, could it only be found. "I am entirely of opinion", she says, "by the Polite Letters I have

[1] Ballard MSS., XLIII, 5.

receiv'd from you that let your employment be what it will you must be a Person of good Birth good Education and an excellent genius.''[1] And what must have convinced him more of the real welcome she gave his friendship, is that she adds, "When you mentioned your early affection for the Study of Antiquities you put me in mind of my Dearest Brother and Tutor".[2]

With this long and interesting letter Elizabeth sends him a transcript from the Saxon, "written I believe by the first Woman that has studied that Language, since it was spoke. I have added a Specimen of Runic, and Gothick should not have been wanting, cou'd I have procur'd it." She asks him to pay her a visit. "You will see a poor little contemptible old maid generally vapour'd up to the ears, but very cheerful when she meets with an agreeable conversation."[3] She shows, in October of the same year, genuine delight at his "obliging design of a visit on Saturday. Not having had", she laments, "for near twenty years the Conversation of one Antiquary."[4] Ballard sends her gifts, and shows his appreciation in every kind of friendly act. In January the next year she speaks of "your most generous Present . . . [probably a "head" from the shop in Campden] you have bestow'd too rich an Ornament upon a head which does not deserve it".[5] And the presents and kindnesses were

[1] Ballard MSS., XLIII, 5.
[2] Ibid., XLIII, 5.
[3] Ibid., XLIII, 5.
[4] Ibid., XLIII, 7.
[5] Ibid., XLIII, 11.

not all on one side; she could make Ballard small, but to him valuable, gifts. Collecting coins was one of his passions and she sends him coins. She could give him help over his projected work on "learned ladies". Volume LXIV of Ballard's Manuscripts in the Bodleian Library consists of a list made by Elizabeth of the names of the learned ladies whom Ballard had chosen. In one or two cases she has written a short account, and spaces are left, that she had obviously meant to fill with information which would help him. The little life of her brother which she sends at his request in January 1736, in her beautiful hand-writing, was probably written earlier, for she says, on March 7, 1736, "it should not so long have continued unprinted had my circumstances been better, or the Booksellers more generous".[1]

She also wrote at his request an account of her own life. This involved an effort of genuine friendship; for on April 10, 1738, she tells him that her "Nervous Fever . . . affects my Head Eyes and Hands so much as to make me almost incapable of writing", and goes on to say: "I will, as soon as possibly I can, endeavour to oblige you . . . by sending some memoirs of my Life, tho' it be an unpleasant task, and what I by no means think a proper one for me."[2] In July she apologizes for not having fulfilled her promise, saying: "I am not able to write with such a Spirit as I could wish, my Mind being as much weakened as my

[1] Ballard MSS., XLIII, 36.
[2] Ibid., XLIII, 51.

Body."[1] But from Bath on November 23, 1738, the little account, formal and condensed, but of great value to us to-day, was finished and sent. "I have", she writes, "at last sent what you so often requested, and what I undertook with so much unwillingness."[2] And she follows this by asking him that if he, as she does from her heart, thinks it is not fit to be communicated, he will commit it to the flames. Ballard, in one of his letters, compared her to an "unfortunate gentlewoman in the past",[3] and in her letter of May 9, 1736, she asks him of whom he was thinking. When he has answered her, she writes on June 15th: "You have put me quite out of Countenance and into the utmost confusion by the great Honour you have done me in comparing me to the incomparable Mrs. Roper, and must therefore pardon me if I chide you for it . . . this last Favour of your accurate account of the Learned Mrs. Margaret Roper will be esteem'd by me as a choice curiosity for which I return you a thousand thanks."[4]

Through Ballard she was brought once more to the notice of scholars and antiquarians, and the overworked, underpaid schoolmistress writes on May 9, 1736: "It has been one of the most agreeable weeks I have known this many years, having had the pleasure of seeing two such valuable persons as Mrs. Chapone and Mr. Parry."[5]

[1] Ballard MSS., XLIII, 54.   [2] Ibid., XLIII, 57.
[3] Ibid., XLIII, 23.   [4] Ibid., XLIII, 25.
[5] For Mr. Parry, see Aubrey's *Letters of Eminent Persons*, Vol. II, p. 133. He is described as "a fellow of Jesus College, famous for caligraphy".

The correspondence between Ballard and Brome and Rawlins, from 1736 to 1738, shows how much Ballard had interested his antiquarian friends in Elizabeth. Brome, who had been one of the original subscribers to her *Homilies of Ælfric*, writes to Rawlins on December 23, 1736, of a letter he has received from Ballard about her. "I hope", he says, "to get somewhat for the poor Saxon Lady, though ours is a bad country for raising contributions. Where *has she spent her time for near twenty years*? for for near that space I have not heard one syllable of her." He adds that he has "under her *fair pretty hand*" on March 13, 1713, a receipt "'Rec. fifteen shillings for one copy of Saxon Homilies. Elizabeth Elstob.' I would give some pounds to pay the other 15s. and have a copy of that fine Book, of which I have a most beautiful specimen."[1]

In January of the next year, 1737, Brome, we find, has collected three guineas for Mrs. Elstob, and has requested Rawlins to deliver them to her by hand. He says that he has not addressed her by name, because "that address might not be proper".[2] Rawlins calls on Elizabeth as requested, and on February 12th gives an account to Ballard of his visit. The subjects touched on in their half-hour's talk must have taken Elizabeth back into the world of scholars that she had left so long. The late loss by fire of the Cottonian Library distressed them both. Rawlins asked her what other works she had published besides

[1] Ballard MSS., XIX, 88.   [2] Ibid., XLI, 130.

the *Homily on St. Gregory's Birthday*. She presented him with a copy of her *English-Saxon Grammar*. And they even discussed the possibility of the production, after all these years, of the book which Rawlins, with all respect, called her "pompous" work, the *Homilies of Ælfric*. Elizabeth's spirit was not broken; "one day or other", she thought, it might be done, meantime she would be content "until that happy time come".[1] Rawlins left, expressing his intention of calling every time he came to Evesham. On March 7, 1737, Elizabeth writes to Ballard that illness had prevented her from writing before, to tell him of this visit, which she owed to his mediation. The only thing that troubled her was the present of three guineas. "It is", she says, "with the greatest trouble imaginable that I receive so many obligations." She asks him not to grieve her in the future in this way. "I think myself sufficiently happy in your Friendship, without any such testimonies."[2] Ballard may have taken her at her obviously sincere word, for we hear no more of subscriptions, but much of their friendship.

Throughout this time, like most people who have been starved for proper human intercourse, she is afraid of talkativeness, now that her thoughts and work have meaning for other people. On March 7, 1736, she says to Ballard: "I fear you will complain, as you have great reason, of the Loquacity of my Pen, for I am like most Bablers, who when they begin know not when to leave off."[3]

[1] Ballard MSS., XLI, 130. [2] Ibid., XLIII, 36. [3] Ibid., XLIII, 18.

Elizabeth had been planning a visit to her ingenuous friend and his mother, the good Mrs. Ballard. More than once it was postponed on the ground of ill-health, but it took place at last early in June 1737. Her letters show that this happy visit was afterwards constantly in her mind. "Since", she says, "it is the first time as far as I can remember that ever I rid five miles to visit a Gentleman, I shall expect the Visit returned."[1] We are grateful to the widowed midwife of Campden, when we hear that she provided Elizabeth with "a vastly kind entertainment . . . I have not", she writes, "these many years (if ever) spent my time more agreeably and more to my real satisfaction".[2] "After I was got safe down the ugly Hill," she says, "I became so courageous that I fear I shall become a troublesome visitor." "I have many things more to add," she goes on, "but my children are all about me."[3] On June 19th she is writing again. Ballard has been ill, and Elizabeth says she has fears that "I might in great measure be the occasion of it by my great impertinence and too much Loquacity". "I do assure you," she says, pathetically, "it is only among those I esteem as my best Friends that I now put on those Gaieties."[4] She remonstrates with Ballard for working too hard, and begs him to imitate her in cheerfulness, "which under God has been the only thing that has kept her alive".[5]

[1] Ballard MSS., XLIII, 42.
[2] Ibid., XLIII, 40.   [3] Ibid., XLIII, 40.
[4] Ibid., XLIII, 42.   [5] Ibid., XLIII, 42.

Although the letters are largely concerned with serious subjects and tell so sad a story, Elizabeth shows in them her lighter side. On December 4, 1736, she is, she says, delighted to hear that "you were so merry at my relation of Mrs. Astell and her Pigeon".[1] Ballard was a friend to whom she could send drawings "imperfect and unfinished, done in my childhood and when a learner".[2] "I sent them to make you laugh, not to be seen by anyone." She not only sends "the Face of Dear Dean Hickes", whose scholarship he well knew, but she thinks he will "not be displeas'd to see the likeness of my good old Grandfather by my Mother's side, the sweetness of whose face shows the goodness of the Man".[3] She sends a drawing of herself, "don't fancy she was ever so handsome, for everyone is apt to be favourable to themselves".[4] She is overcome with modesty when she finds that he has shown her drawings to his friends. For Ballard had sent them to his great friend Brome, who was much impressed. In April 1738 Brome writes asking if he may see the account of her Life done by her own pen. "No person", he says, "can have a greater esteem for her than I have, and more admire her Pen, and now I may say Pencill."[5] Elizabeth had drawn a portrait of Ballard, of which he makes a present to Brome. Brome refers more than once to Ballard as Elizabeth's "gladiator", and when Ballard sends him her

---

[1] Ballard MSS., XLIII, 31.
[2] Ibid., XLIII, 42.
[3] Ibid., XLIII, 42.
[4] Ibid., XLIII, 42.
[5] Ibid., XLI, 20.

portraits of Dryden and Ogilvy, which were to be returned, he asked Brome to keep the one of himself that came with them. For Brome in April 1738 speaks of Elizabeth's "gladiator" as amongst his greatest rarities, and in July he writes: "I am afraid you plundered yourself too much by bestowing the 3rd upon me, but it is transferred into Hands that sett a great and true value upon it."[1] In the same letter he speaks of "the excellent Pencil that drew such a Champion for Gratitude".[2]

George Ballard was essentially modest, and he must have felt real pleasure when Elizabeth wrote to him that his conversation and friendship had "saved a gentlewoman from lethargy".[3] But such pleasures could not save the elderly woman from growing ill-health and fear of a destitute future. Even in January 1736, when she sends Ballard the short account of her brother's life in her still beautiful handwriting, she apologizes for it, asking him to consider "that it is drawn up by one who has had many things to destroy her Memory, and had no assistance to do it but that bad Memory".[4] In the account of her own life, that she writes for him later, she says: "I am unable to write with such a Spirit as I could wish, my Mind being as much weaken'd as my Body."[5]

It is not surprising that while Elizabeth was keeping her school in Evesham, her friends were trying to

---

[1] Ballard MSS., XLI, 21.
[2] Ibid., XLI, 21.
[3] Ibid., XLIII, 42.
[4] Ibid., XLIII, 11.
[5] Ibid., XLIII, 53.

find work for her that would be less "precarious and fatiguing". When the correspondence with Ballard opens, the indefatigable Mrs. Chapone had approached Lady Elizabeth Hastings, through Mr. Hastings, a gentleman whom, she says, "Lady Betty Hastings honours with her friendship",[1] to get for Elizabeth the head mistresship of the charity school that Lady Betty Hastings was at that time starting. Mrs. Chapone was very hopeful; for on January 13, 1736, Elizabeth tells Ballard that she has received "a most affectionate and ingenious letter from the excellent Mrs. Chapone", in which she is "very pressing for my acceptance of this Proposal".[2] This ingenious letter is fortunately preserved, and Sarah Chapone can speak for herself. On January 11, 1736, she writes: "I return'd from Evesham the day after I had had the pleasure of your Conversation, fully Determin'd to endeavour to do you some Service. I could think of no method so likely to succeed as getting Lady Betty Hastings inform'd that you were still living.—I think it is the most eligible thing that could happen to you." Mrs. Chapone goes on to say that there will be an annual income, and that "in case of sickness or disability to take care of the School I suppose you might be certain of the Favour and Protection of the worthy foundress, who, I persuade myself, could never see a Person of your Merit in distress without endeavouring to soften it by the tenderest humanity and compassion". She thinks

[1] Ballard MSS., XLIII, 19.   [2] Ibid., XLIII, 11.

Elizabeth, in her present situation, is neglected because few people know her worth; "Conversation being the proper entertainment of a thinking Person, and you can find no companions suitable to your Taste and Learning. These uneasinesses would be all removed if you were near Lady Betty." Lady Betty would reward Elizabeth Elstob's merit, "an happiness too great for me to enjoy or I should refer it to no other Person breathing, a pretty large Family and a Precarious Fortune leaves me little room for generosity, except it be that of the Heart".[1] Sarah's heart deserved the capital letter she gave it, and although she may have been too optimistic about the amount of time Lady Betty would have been able to give to "enlightened conversation" with the mistress of her charity school, Lady Betty's record makes it almost certain that if she had employed Elizabeth she would never have let her want.

Ballard had obviously objected in one of his letters to Mrs. Elstob's acceptance of the mistresship of a charity school. "As to your objection", she writes on March 7, 1736, "of the Meanness of the Scholars, I assure you I should think it as Glorious an Employment to Instruct those Poor Children as to teach the Children of the Greatest Monarch."[2] But she has a fear which she confides to Ballard that she is not really fitted for this work. "There are some things to be taught in such a school", her letter goes on to say, "which I cannot pretend to. I mean the two Accom-

---

[1] Ballard MSS., XLIII, 19.   [2] Ibid., XLIII, 17.

plishments of a good House-wife, Spinning and Knitting. Not that I w'd be thought to be above doing any commendable Work proper for my sex, for I have continually in my thoughts, the Glorious Character of a Virtuous Woman (Prov. xxxi. 13), 'She seeketh wool and Flax and worketh willingly with her hands'." In proof of this she tells him that the gown she had on when he gave her the "favour of a Visit" was, part of it, her own spinning, "and I wear no other Stockings but what I knitt myself".[1]

But even Mrs. Chapone's letters were not always successful; and although Mr. Hastings, in writing to Mrs. Chapone on January 6, 1736, tells her that the "lively manner" in which she had "pointed" Mrs. Elstob's "distress"[2] had made him depart from his general rule and actually write to Lady Betty about Mrs. Elstob, Elizabeth tells Ballard on March 7, 1736, that "hearing no more of that affair makes me think her Ladyship is provided with a mistress before now".[3] Mrs. Chapone had done her best, and the disappointment did not prevent Elizabeth from enjoying this "valuable" woman's conversation. The visit Mrs. Chapone paid her on May 9, 1736, was, she tells Ballard, "all too short. Still I have the pleasure of reflecting on every word she said, which will be an agreeable entertainment, for my private thoughts, until it shall please God to afford me such another satisfaction."[4] For a year or two after this Elizabeth's

[1] Ballard MSS., XLIII, 17.
[2] Ibid., XLIII, 21.
[3] Ibid., XLIII, 21.
[4] Ibid., XLIII, 23.

health grew steadily worse. By October 1738 she has decided to give up her School in the High Street, and the children of Evesham were no longer to receive their education from a trained scholar in the Northern languages.

Elizabeth must have suffered from an acute form of rheumatism which eventually crippled her hands. Often during her later years one of her pupils acts as her "scribe", and improvement in her handwriting always indicates an improvement in health. Bath waters were the accepted treatment for rheumatism, and her friends most likely offered to make it possible for her to settle and seek work in Bath. She writes to Ballard on October 10, 1738, about this plan. "It will be almost Death to me to go so far from my excellent Friends", but her decision was made. "Being assured . . . that the Bath is the only place in the world to settle in, not only on account of my health, but on account of my affairs also, having an indefatigable Friend a Person of Honour to recommend me." She is, she says, to set out "on Thursday next, that I may be there before the roads are too bad".[1] The change may have done good to her health, although she was ill during her stay, but from the point of view of her affairs, Bath was a disappointment. She writes to Ballard on November 22, 1738, that although she had been "most zealously recommended by Dear Mrs. Pendarves, Miss Granville and Mrs. Chapone to several Persons of Worth and Honour", she had so

[1] Ballard MSS., XLIII, 55.

far had nothing but "discouragements and disappointments".[1] She also speaks of an "ugly fever" that will stick to her. But at Bath she meets kindness and friendship from a man who understands a little what she is aiming at. "He has been", she tells Ballard, "an extraordinary Friend to me and will I daresay be the same still as far as is in his power. He is one of the most Eminent Physicians here. He tells me mine is a wrong employment to hope for any encouragement in, if I cou'd teach to make Artificial Flowers, a bit of Tapistry, and the like I shou'd get more than I shall by instilling the Principles of Religion and Virtue, or improving the Minds of Young Ladies, for those are things little regarded."[2]

Not two months after this letter Elizabeth begins to have a new hope for the future. Mrs. Delany had been trying to place her as governess to the infant children of her friend Margaret, Duchess of Portland—the "Noble lovely little Peggy"—to whom, when a child, Prior addressed a poem, exhorting her to be obedient to her parents, and to say her morning and evening prayers first in English and then in French. Sally Chapone's pen was once more brought into use. Mrs. Delany thought it well to show the Duchess a copy of the letter that had so touched Queen Caroline's heart. "When I see the Duchess of Portland," she writes to her sister, "I shall have Sally's historic epistle."[3] On

[1] Ballard MSS., XLIII, 57.
[2] Ibid., XLIII, 57. November 22, 1738.
[3] Delany, *Autobiography*, II, p. 31.

December 12, 1738, it was still very uncertain whether
Mrs. Elstob would obtain this post. Mrs. Delany
writes that the Duchess has "a thousand fears" about
it, "lest my Lord and Lady Oxford [her father and
mother] should have any objections against taking
her, but I hope they will all prove false".[1] Mrs.
Elstob, "out of modesty and diffidence of herself", it
was thought, might decline the offer. At this time
the Granville sisters, though so active on Mrs. Elstob's
behalf, did not know her personally. "I own", writes
Mrs. Delany to Anne Dewes, "I long to have you *see
her*, that I may really know what sort of woman she
is."[2] One of Lord Oxford's objections was that Mrs.
Elstob did not speak French. But Mrs. Delany writes
on December 12, 1738, that the Duchess will arrange
to have a master or a maid to talk with the children,
and that "all she requires or hopes of Mrs. Elstob is
to instruct her children in the principles of religion
and virtue, to teach them to speak read and understand English well, to cultivate their minds as far as
their capacity will allow, and to keep them company
in the house, and when her strength and health will
permit take the air with them. All this she is surely
well qualified to do, and it would be a sincere joy to
me to have our worthy Duchess possest of so valuable
a person, but don't speak of her coming here till 'tis
more confirmed."[3]

Elizabeth's scruples were overcome; she thought

[1] Delany, *Autobiography*, II, p. 14.
[2] Ibid., II, p. 14.   [3] Ibid., IV, p. 14.

herself equal to these duties; and by December 22nd Mrs. Delany writes, "the Elstobian affair is quite fixed". The Duchess had expressed the "utmost satisfaction" at securing her. Her salary was to be £30 a year, and the Duchess arranged that payment should begin on Christmas Day, although she thought she would not want Mrs. Elstob until Midsummer. Mrs. Delany tells her sister that she has given Mrs. Elstob "a little hint", and she expresses her approval of Mrs. Dewes having lost no time in advising Mrs. Elstob to pay her debts. "A person of such principles as hers", she says, "cannot enjoy advantages without doing that justice when it is in her power to do it."[1] The Duchess's arrangement was thoughtful and generous for the period in which she lived, and Mrs. Elstob's debts must have been small if they could be discharged by what was left from £15 after provision for her support for six months.

Great interest was felt among her friends when the news of her engagement with the Duchess was known. Elizabeth's own delight when she had decided to accept the offer was unbounded. For twenty-four years she had known grinding poverty, ill-deserved shame, and fear for her future. Now she had found security and work. On January 3, 1739, she writes to Ballard, "Neither my Best Friends nor myself could have wish'd for a more happy and Honourable situation for me".[2] Mrs. Delany, of course, was

[1] Delany, *Autobiography*, II, p. 18.
[2] Ballard MSS., XLIII, 61.

delighted. No doubt seems to have entered her mind whether the "possession" of this "valuable woman" was the best possible arrangement for the Duchess. "Lady Betty", she writes to her sister, "is rather too young to have a preceptor, being but three years, but as Mrs. Elstob has no settled home to go to, I daresay the Duchess will consent to take her before the time of being wanted. I much fear her being in so bad a state of health will make her incapable of application." "But", she adds, "being settled in a good family where she will have no cares, may be more beneficial to her than all the physicians."[1]

The only note of doubt of the suitability of the post for Mrs. Elstob comes from Brome, the antiquarian, who, writing to Rawlins on March 3, 1739, expresses pleasure but some surprise at the appointment. He had known her in her youth, and evidently thinks that her character will make such a position as the one she was going to occupy in the Portland family not entirely suitable for her. He is delighted, he says, "to hear that the Saxon Lady is to leave Evesham for a better Place. I hope she has seen so much of the world, as since her Dedication of A. S. Grammer, she may have other thoughts; but if they should continue *the same*, desire her, conjure her to secret them."[2] Thinking probably of Mrs. Delany's early friendship with Swift, he says such ideas "will be displeasing to the Great Lady's Friends; with whom I have the

[1] Delany, *Autobiography*, II, p. 33.
[2] Ballard MSS., XIX, 141.

honour to be intimately acquainted; and have such an interest in, that I could render her stay precarious; which I am so far from doing that I send this caution to make her settlement there the more firm". Later in the letter he writes: "What I wrote about the Saxon Lady was out of plenitude of respect for her; if your discretion judge silence more proper, then let my good intentions go no further than yourself."[1] Brome was genuine in his desire to help her, for Elizabeth, in a letter to Ballard from Whitehall in June 1740, asks Ballard to thank "our Worthy Friend Mr. Brome" for the "good offices he had been pleased to do me with Mr. Edward Harley". She had already thanked Brome, but says: "I think it cannot be done too often, because it has given satisfaction to her Grace."[2]

From Bath, before entering the Duchess's family, Elizabeth went back to Evesham, probably to settle up her small affairs, and the last we hear of her life in Evesham is when she writes to Ballard of an "exceeding pleasure" she had experienced. She had a visit from Mrs. Chapone, and had listened, not without concern, to a dispute between her "dear and valuable" friend and Mr. Ben Seward. It was on "some methodistical notions" of his, and we are not surprised when Mrs. Elstob says, "the *female* antagonist had much the advantage over him".[3]

On January 26, 1739, when Elizabeth had already

[1] Ballard MSS., XIX, 141.   [2] Ibid., XLIII, 67.
[3] Delany, *Autobiography*, II, p. 85.

begun work with the Portland family, she writes to
George Ballard: "To give you an account of all her
Grace's accomplishments and Perfections is more than
I can possibly do, and shou'd be done by a much
better hand." "I must now beg leave to say something
of my charming little Pupils, whose Persons, Sweet
Temper and Good Sense, plainly discover whose
offspring they are."[1] The ages of the pupils of Mrs.
Elstob, whose natural companions were antiquaries
and scholars, were three, two, and, if we count the
little Marquis, one year old. After she entered the
family, two more children were born, one of whom
died in infancy.

The children's welcome warmed Mrs. Elstob's
heart. Even the little Marquis stretched out his arms
to her and called her "Tob".[2] On May 6, 1740,
nearly eighteen months later, she writes to Miss
Granville of Lady Betty, then four years old: "She
learns exceedingly well, and loves her book and me
entirely; nor is she ever more happy than when she
is with me and we study together, even to candle
light, like two old folks."[3] In November, Lady Betty,
writing to her "Dear Pip" (Mrs. Dewes), gives an
account of her own studies; she tells her: "I learn very
well the Common Prayer book and Bible, and have
almost got by heart the Turtle and Sparrow." She
had also learnt "Molly Mog of the Rose, and am

---

[1] Ballard MSS., XLIII, 67.
[2] Delany, *Autobiography*, II, p. 67.
[3] Ibid., II, p. 35.

learning now the English grammar".[1] Writing to Miss
Granville from Whitehall on Christmas Day, 1739,
Elizabeth speaks of "my happiness", and "the incom-
parable author of it, the not to be paralleled Mrs.
Pendarves".[2]

At first, in the kindly atmosphere of her welcome,
Elizabeth evidently hoped that the generosity which
she had received from the Portland family might be
extended to her friends. In the letter to Ballard of
January 26, 1739, she says: "I had like to have forgot
to acquaint you with the incomparable Mrs. Pendarves' goodness. . . . I had not been with her
above an hour before she enquir'd after you, in a most
sweet manner, and I am apt to believe it is she that
has mention'd you to the Duchess, and I did not
forget to tell them both who it was that made my
Brown Gown, which was commend'd by them both."[3]
"Let me know", she writes, "in what I can serve you
to your best liking, for unless I know that I shall be
at a loss what to ask for from her Grace."[4] She evidently hopes that the Duchess will be of use to her
friend, not simply as a maker of gowns, but as a
scholar. But Elizabeth had to learn (as Fanny Burney
learnt when, forty-six years later, the same Mrs.
Delany placed her in the household of the Queen),
that eighteenth-century great ladies were made wary
by the constant appeals which they had to meet.
Even in the same letter she says: "It happen'd so

---

[1] Delany, *Autobiography*, II, p. 131.   [2] Ibid., II, p. 67.
[3] Ballard MSS., XLIII, 67.   [4] Ibid., XLIII, 67.

unluckily that when we have just been going to talk
of you, and I with joy hop'd an opportunity had presented itself for me to do you service, some body or
other has come in, and put a stop to our discourse and
my happiness". Still, she is "not without great hopes
that I shall some time or other have an opportunity
which may be proper to say something in your
favour".[1]

As early as May 1740, when she wrote to Miss
Granville so happily of Lady Betty, she was feeling
that she saw very little of Mrs. Delany and the
Duchess. "I want nothing here to make my happiness complete as this world can make it but the
pleasure of seeing Mrs. Pendarves oftener, who is
entirely engrossed by her Grace."[2] She is anxious to
go from Whitehall to Bulstrode, where, she says, "I
hope I shall have the honour of more of her Grace's
company for it is impossible to have any of it here".[3]
But at Bulstrode the life of the governess in the
nursery was very much what it had been at Whitehall.
Even such a pleasure as she had had at Evesham, of
listening to Mrs. Chapone in a theological argument,
could not happen again. Mrs. Chapone was not in
the social position to be one of the Duchess's guests at
Bulstrode, and she had a year earlier distressed her
friend Mrs. Delany by her tactlessness in suggesting
that Mrs. Delany while at Bulstrode should ask her
to spend a week there and should introduce her to the

[1] Ballard MSS., XLIII, 67.
[2] Delany, *Autobiography*, II, pp. 35–56.   [3] Ibid., II, p. 56.

Duchess. "Alas," Mrs. Delany writes to her sister, "how wild is imagination when let loose, and not trimmed by *a little knowledge of the world*. . . . I have written her plainly *the impossibility* of putting such a scheme in practice."[1] When Elizabeth had only been at Bulstrode about twelve months she writes to Ballard in October 1740, "I have less time than I ever had in my life to command because it is not my own";[2] and towards the end of her life she writes to him: "Alas, my acquaintance and interest is reduced to a very narrow compass".[3]

As far as we know, Elizabeth and George Ballard only met once during the seventeen years that she lived with the Portland family. From 1750 until his death in 1754 Ballard was living in bad health at Oxford. During the last ten years of his life he was struggling to bring out his *Memoirs of Learned Ladies*. There is no evidence that he himself ever asked Elizabeth to do anything for him; but Mrs. Chapone tells him on May 30, 1745, that she had written to Mrs. Elstob to ask her to use her influence to obtain leave for him to dedicate his book to "her Grace of Portland", and quotes the letter she received in answer. Mrs. Elstob says: "She is not sensible that she has any particular interest [i.e. influence], having taken all opportunities of mentioning you to her Grace, in hopes she would express a desire to promote you. She tells me I had better apply to Mrs. Delany,

---

[1] Delany, *Autobiography*, II, p. 15.
[2] Ballard MSS., XLIII, 70.
[3] Ibid., XLIII, 57.

to obtain her Grace's Patronage." Then later: "She [Mrs. Elstob] desires her affectionate service to you, and quite condoles herself that she can give you no other testimony of her regard. I know her benevolent heart would rejoice to serve, either you or me," but, she adds, and it is sad that the exuberant Mrs. Chapone had learnt her lesson, too, "the influence of the most worthy person, extends but a little way unless supported by Title and Fortune".[1]

In a letter, about the same time, to Ballard, on the subject of the publication of his book, Elizabeth warns him that in the great houses even of enlightened people, the idea that women should undertake serious intellectual work is unpopular. "I am sorry to tell you", she says, "the choice you have made for the Honour of the Females was the wrongest subject you could pitch upon. For you can come into no company of Ladies and Gentlemen, where you shall not hear an open and vehement exclamation against Learned Women, and by those women who read much themselves, to what purposes they know best. . . . The prospect I have of the next age is a melancholy one to me who wish Learning might flourish to the end of the World, both in Men and Women, but I shall not live to see it."[2] But although Elizabeth cannot use influence with the Duchess on Ballard's behalf, she shows active sympathy in the difficulties, which she knew only too well, of publishing by subscription. In spite of ill-health and crippled hands, she writes letters

[1] Ballard MSS., XLIII, 142.   [2] Ibid., XLIII, 89.

begging for subscriptions, and the Duchess of Portland
with her three daughters are among the list of subscribers for one copy each. When the book appeared,
the dedication was not to the Duchess. The first part
was dedicated to Ballard's friend, Mrs. Talbot; the
second, probably through Sally Chapone's efforts,
to Mrs. Delany.

When Ballard died, Mrs. Elstob had survived the
only friend who could have written, from his own
knowledge, an appreciative account of her life and
work. Nichols, in his *Literary Anecdotes*, is contented
with the description of Elizabeth Elstob which Dr.
Lightfoot had given him on the authority of the
Duchess, who had told him that in her later years
Mrs. Elstob, "though very agreeable in her temper
and conversation was a remarkably plain woman";
and also that she lived "with cheerfulness and *great
approbation* in her family to the end".[1] For further
knowledge of Elizabeth's last years we have to rely
almost wholly on Mrs. Delany's correspondence.
This, unfortunately, shows a growing strain in Elizabeth's relations with the friends to whom she owed
her post. The troubles that arose were, as Brome had
foreseen, natural enough where a woman of Elizabeth
Elstob's character and attainments lived, as a dependent, in the complex society of an eighteenth-century
"great house". It is sad to find, in her later letters from
Bulstrode, a note of bitterness that was absent when
the subject of her hopes and prayers was her daily

[1] Nichols's *Literary Anecdotes*, IV, 714.

bread. Mrs. Delany's letters tell of Elizabeth's health
and anxieties towards the end of her life. On December 9, 1753, she says: "I am just come down from
Mrs. Elstob. She is wrapt up in her young lords and
ladies, and I believe has no thoughts of quitting them
till they disperse into homes of their own; and indeed
she is too infirm to undertake any fresh charge now."[1]
On October 25th of the next year, 1754, she writes to
her sister: "Mrs. Elstob is as well as she can expect to
be, but very uneasy that she cannot write to you, but
her fingers are so contracted she cannot guide a pen."
The next reference to Elizabeth is eighteen months
later, when, on April 20, 1756, the Duchess of Portland was in grave anxiety; for Margaret Bentinck,
the baby born a few months before Mrs. Elstob came
into the family, was seriously ill, and died on April 28,
1756. "Mrs. Elstob, you may imagine, has her share
of complaints, but, poor woman, she feels so much for
herself, that she does not seem to think others as bad
as they really are, and indeed everybody makes the
best of it *to her*."[2] A month later, on May 24th, Mrs.
Delany writes, "Mrs. Elstob is gradually drawing
towards that happy repose which we may presume so
good a woman may obtain".[3]

Elizabeth was evidently in a difficult state of mind
at this time. On one point she even disregarded the
Duchess's wishes. On May 24, 1756, Mrs. Delany
writes to Mrs. Dewes: "I have made her many visits

[1] Delany, *Autobiography*, III, p. 253.
[2] Ibid., III, p. 422.   [3] Ibid., III, pp. 428–429.

during my constant attendance at Whitehall, and urged her as the Duchess desired me, to have some physician." Mrs. Elstob refused: "She said she had a better opinion of Dr. Groat than any of them, and would have none." But there was a worse trouble. In the same letter Mrs. Delany says that Mrs. Elstob "never desires any clergyman to come to her"; and she turned in her last days to her own relations. A cousin Mallet visited her very often, who was, Mrs. Delany writes, "a Roman Catholic". This lady brought Elizabeth "presents of chocolate, and seems to pay great court to her".

It is little wonder that Mrs. Delany, who had always thought of Elizabeth's relation to the Duchess as a means of advancing the interests of Sally Chapone, now begins to fear that Sally may not benefit by Mrs. Elstob's will. In this letter, written shortly before Elizabeth's death, Mrs. Delany tells her sister that Mrs. Elstob is already so ill as to be unable at first to recognize her. She hopes that "if the poor woman has any little sum she will bestow it on *the friend* who was the *first* occasion of her being brought out of obscurity; but I fear she is out of favour, and I don't know in a letter how to tell you the particulars about it"[1]. Mrs. Chapone appears never to have asked favours for herself, and her references to Elizabeth are always warm and friendly. As late as April 1749 she writes to Ballard: "I visited our dear Mrs. Elstob last summer at Bulstrode. . . . Mrs. Elstob has no more than a

[1] Delany, *Autobiography*, III, pp. 428–429.

tolerable share of health, but she bears all things nobly."[1]

On June 23, 1756, Mrs. Elstob died. Her death, Mrs. Delany thinks, was hastened by the news of Lady Margaret's death, so that it may have been good sense as well as kindness on the part of the Duchess and her family to keep their anxiety as far as possible from her. When Elizabeth was either dying or dead (a confusion as to the date makes it difficult to decide which) Mrs. Delany writes again. "I am afraid", she says, "Mrs. Elstob has not remembered her chief friend Mrs. Chapone, as she has taken an unreasonable prejudice to her, and spoke of it not only to the Duchess and the young ones, but to Mr. Achard. I am sorry she never mentioned it to me, I could have set her right, but so far from seeming to take anything ill she always joined me in commending her. I suppose she cannot have left much money; seventy guineas were found, but whether she has any stock of any kind cannot be known till her papers are enquired into." This, she says, was to be done as soon as Mrs. Mallet and her sister Mrs. Elstob (her two nearest relations) could come to look over them with the Duke's agent. It is clear that Elizabeth had at the end no one at Bulstrode in whom she cared to confide. Mrs. Delany knew later whether she had held a little stock, and, if so, in what way she disposed of it and of her few possessions. But there is no further mention of the subject in Mrs. Delany's letters, and we shall

[1] Ballard MSS., XLIII, 145.

probably never know what became of the seventy guineas which the old scholar had saved.

There was beyond a doubt a happier side to Elizabeth Elstob's later life, if only we had more knowledge of it. In December 1754 Mrs. Dewes speaks of her as "very lame in her hands", but of her mind as being "as free and exalted as possible", and to the very end she was devoted to the children she had taught. A letter from Elizabeth on March 24, 1753, to Mrs. Dewes shows that, in spite of the very modest demands which the Duchess had originally made on her attainments, Elizabeth, as the children grew up, still felt herself in some degree responsible for their education. Of the Marquis of Titchfield she writes: "*I can safely say without boasting* or partiality, *he is an admirable scholar* for his age, which is not fifteen until the middle of next month."[1] The younger boy, Lord Edward, who was just going to Westminster, she speaks of as "a delightful little man" of whom she was "only too fond". If the elders at Bulstrode had no place in their crowded lives for Elizabeth's best gifts of scholarship, the children at any rate must have gained much from her methods and from the character that had made her scholarship possible. And in the generosity of their youth her knowledge, her high standard of workmanship, and her unbroken spirit, may have made a lasting impression.

[1] Delany, *Autobiography*, III, p. 215.

THE DEBT OF WOMEN TO
SIR RICHARD STEELE

CHAPTER VI

THE DEBT OF WOMEN TO
SIR RICHARD STEELE

THE publication, on April 12, 1709, of the first number of the *Tatler*, by Captain Richard Steele, whose immediate object was to pay his debts, is an important event in the history of literature. But it is also important in the history of social life in England and particularly in the social life of women. The credit of the success of the *Tatler* and its successor, the *Spectator*, was given throughout the eighteenth and the first half of the nineteenth centuries, almost entirely to Addison; and Steele encouraged that idea. But the gradual change of literary and social perspective in the years since Steele's death has given fresh emphasis to the importance, not only for his contemporaries, but for ourselves, of his share in the joint work.

Steele, in one of his last contributions to the *Spectator*, says: "I claim to myself the Merit of having extorted excellent Productions from a Person of the greatest Abilities, who would not have let them appear by any other Means" (*Spectator*, 351).

But while Steele turned Addison's wise eyes and trained mind from the study of classical antiquities to the England of his day, the truth is that no two people ever gained more by collaboration, than did Addison and Steele in the three years and nine months during

N

which, inspired by a rare friendship, they produced true literature in popular periodical form.

The amazing success of the *Tatler* began while Addison was still in Ireland, and before he had contributed largely to it. From its first number, Steele was conscious of a new public, for whom he wrote and with whom he kept in touch to the end of his connection with the *Spectator*. This public was largely composed of the increasing middle class, who liked their reading to be neither smutty nor pedantic, who were not interested in the rancour of political parties or the intolerance of religious bodies. They, and especially the women among them, suffered directly from the immorality and extravagance made fashionable by the habits of the small ruling class.

Steele's recognition of women as an integral part of the reading-public was entirely new, and is one of the chief causes of the immediate popularity of the *Tatler* and the *Spectator*. Religious bodies had made great efforts to rouse their members to the spiritual and physical dangers of the prevailing low standard of morals. But their influence was weakened by divisions among themselves, and by fear of the "wits", who mercilessly attacked those predecessors of the Methodists who could be accused of "enthusiasm". This fear of the "wits" is found throughout the serious writings of the time. A group of men, generally representing the interest of the reigning political party, wielded a power, in the small London of the eighteenth century, that it is difficult for us to understand. If a man's views gave offence, his chance of a living might be destroyed by a jest, and a woman's reputation was apt to suffer equally, whether she offended by her prudery or by her want of it.

The editors of the *Tatler* and the *Spectator*, who like the religious leaders were on the side of simplicity in life and restraint in morals, had no fear of the "wits"; for between them they had wit enough and to spare. Up to this time the champions of decent living had defended it with heavy guns; Steele and Addison skirmished with the light weapon of laughter, and against them the follies of what they called "Fop men" and "Fop women" had no means of defence.

Gay[1] tells us of the "infinite surprize of all men" when, the *Tatler* being at the height of its popularity, "Mr. Steele flung it up, at the beginning of winter"; and then, in one of the finest tributes a man ever paid to a contemporary, Gay says:[2] "It is incredible to conceive the effect his writings have had on the town . . . how entirely they have convinced our fops and young fellows of the value and advantages of learning. . . ." "His Writings", he says again, "have set all our Wits and Men of Letters upon a new way of Thinking. . . . I think we may venture to affirm, that every one of them Writes and Thinks much more justly than they did some time since."

Perhaps Steele's rarest gift, a gift that Charles Lamb alone among English writers possesses in anything like the same degree, was that of establishing with his

[1] Gay, *The Present State of Wit* (1711).   [2] Ibid., p. 254.

readers a relationship that has in it something of actual friendship. Hazlitt tells us how his own loneliness and disillusionment were cheered by Steele's writing "when the tomes of casuistry and ecclesiastical history, with which the little duodecimo volumes of the *Tatler* were overwhelmed and surrounded in the only library to which I had access as a boy, had tried their tranquilising effect in vain". After a fine appreciation of the work both of Addison and Steele, in which, perhaps for the first time since Gay wrote his *Present State of Wit*, Steele is justly estimated, Hazlitt says: "I owed this acknowledgment to a writer who has so often put me in good humour with myself, and everything about me, when few things else could."[1] And what Steele could give Hazlitt, he gave in full measure to his contemporaries, and particularly to the women. It was the first time that a man with rare gifts of imagination and sympathy had recognized in popular writing the unity of the interests of men and women in all the chief concerns of life.

"Literature", Steele wrote in *Tatler* 197, "does but make a Man more eminently what Nature made him." The philosopher, George Berkeley, afterwards Bishop of Cloyne, in 1713, when he was a young man of twenty-eight, visited Steele. In their talk together Steele told Berkeley that he had just inherited £500 a year, and, also, that "this addition to his fortune would rather encourage him to exert himself more than ever". Berkeley adds, "I am apter to

[1] On the Periodical Essayists (1819), pp. 194, 195.

believe him because there appears in his natural
temper something very generous and a great benevolence to mankind".[1] It was in no ordinary measure
that Steele was benevolent; with him sympathy was
a dominant quality and pity a passion. He was aware
of his unusual sensibility to suffering, and was by no
means proud of it. When he was not quite five years
old his father died, and he tells us of the effect produced on his mind by his mother's grief. "I went
into the Room," he says, "where his Body lay, and
my Mother sat weeping alone by it. I had my Battle-
dore in my Hand, and fell abeating the Coffin, and
calling Papa; for, I know not how, I had some slight
Idea that he was locked up there." This childish
action broke up "the silent Grief" that his mother
had been in, and she caught him in her arms and
wept. "Hence it is", he says, "that Good Nature in
me is no Merit: but having been so frequently overwhelmed with her Tears before I knew Cause of
any Affliction, or could draw Defences from my own
Judgment, I imbibed Commiseration, Remorse, and
an unmanly Gentleness of Mind which has since
ensnared me into Ten Thousand Calamities" (*Tatler*,
181).

If to a lively compassion for the sorrows of others
Steele owed ten thousand calamities, yet there is no
other record of a man's sympathy with his fellows
adding so largely to his own capacity for happiness.
When Steele sits reading the life of some man who,

[1] Aitken, *Life of Steele*, Vol. I, p. 360.

after struggles with prejudice and envy, reaches the
"Splendor of Success", he tells us, "I close my Book,
and am an happy Man for a whole Evening". He
explains that his own "Circumstances are indeed so
narrow and scanty" that he would not have much
enjoyment were it not that, owing to a "great Tincture
of Humanity" . . . "every Man who does himself
any real Service, does me a Kindness". (*Tatler*, 117).
In the account of *A Ramble from Richmond to
London*, he tells us that he had resolved on reaching
London "to walk it out of Cheapness". But he recon-
siders this because, as he explains, "my unhappy
Curiosity is such I find it always my Interest to take
Coach; for some odd Adventure among Beggars,
Ballad-Singers or the like, detains and throws me
into Expence".

But with this precaution against immediately
emptying his purse, how he enjoyed himself! "As I
drove along," he writes, "it was a pleasing Reflection
to see the World so prettily chequered, since I left
Richmond, and the Scene still filling with Children
of a new Hour." When he reaches the City the "Children of a new Hour" are the "Merchants on Change".
"I, indeed," he says, "look'd upon myself as the
richest Man that was on the Exchange that day; for
my Benevolence made me share the Gains of every
Bargain that was made" (*Spectator*, 454).

Whenever Steele's imagination is fired to this
point by his amazing sympathy, he attains his best
literary effects. The characters of the "club", which

gives the special note to the *Spectator*, were invented by Steele, and sketched by him in the second number. The first of them is that of the gentleman "very singular in his Behaviour", with the singularities, we are told, that "proceed from his good Sense", our much-loved Sir Roger de Coverley.

It was Addison who developed and made perfect the quaint picture of an English Squire, old-fashioned in 1711, yet living to-day. It is he who describes Sir Roger at church, "surprised into a short Nap at Sermon", but who, when he awakes and "sees any Body else nodding either wakes them himself, or sends his Servants to them". It is Addison's Sir Roger who explains to his guest how he had chosen his chaplain, and that he had been "afraid of being insulted with Latin and Greek at his own Table; for which Reason, he desired a particular Friend of his at the University to find out a Clergyman rather of plain Sense than too much Learning", and who was to be "of a good Aspect, a clear Voice, a sociable Temper, and, if possible, a Man that understood a little of Back-Gammon" (*Spectator*, 106). But Steele, who originally created Sir Roger, endears his character to us. It is through Steele that Sir Roger says, in speaking of his hopeless passion for his widow: "It is, perhaps, to this dear Image in my Heart owing, that I am apt to relent, that I easily forgive, and that many desirable things are grown into my Temper, which I should not have arrived at by better Motives than the Thought of being one Day hers" (*Spectator*,

118). As an illustration of "these desirable things that had grown into his temper", Steele tells us of Sir Roger's conduct towards his old servants. Sir Roger thought that it was not enough to be merely bountiful to them. It was his opinion, Steele says, that "a Man of Honour and Generosity considers it would be miserable to himself to have no Will, but that of another, tho' it were of the best Person breathing, and for that Reason, goes on as fast as he is able to put his Servants into independent Livelihoods".

As scenes from the daily life of his time, those dealing with Mr. Bickerstaffe's half-sister Jenny, in the *Tatler*, are among Steele's best writings. Jenny was a wit, and Mr. Bickerstaffe admits that she was in consequence "a little but a very little, sluttish". But he does not, on account of her being a wit, hold her up as an object of ridicule; he takes a certain pride in her parts. Jenny, he tells us, "instead of consulting her Glass, and her Toilet for an Hour and an Half after her private Devotions", sits "with her Nose full of Snuff, and a Man's Night-Cap on her Head, reading Plays and Romances". He adds: "It would make you laugh to see me often with my Spectacles on, lacing her Stays, for she is so very a Wit, that she understands no ordinary Thing in the World" (*Tatler*, 75).

As a good brother of his day it is his business to procure a husband for her. She is, he claims, "as unspotted a Spinster as any in Great Britain", and the fact that she is "so very a Wit" does not, in his

eyes, unfit her for marriage, but makes it desirable
that she should have a husband of sound judgment.
This being so, he fixes his choice on the "honest
Tranquillus", and on the eve of Jenny's marriage he
talks to her, while she, "having her Heart full of the
great Change of Life from a virgin Condition to that
of a wife, long sat silent. . . . 'Sister' (said I) 'you
are now going from me. . . . But take this along
with you, That there is no Mean in the State you are
entering into . . . and your Fortune in this Way of
Life will be wholly of your own making.' "

His immediate advice is that she should have a
good bath and drop the habit of snuff taking. "When",
he tells her, "two Persons have so good an Opinion
of each as to come together for Life they will not
differ in Matters of Importance." "In all the Marriages I have ever seen (most of which have been
unhappy ones) the great Cause of Evil has proceeded
from slight Occasions; and I take it to be the first
Maxim in a married Condition, that you are to be
above Trifles."

To impress on her the need in married life of
good will and patience in little things, he tells the
tragic story of Sir Harry Willit and his Lady. Sir
Harry one day was reading a grave author and his
wife "runs into his Study and in a playing Humour,
claps the Squirrel upon the Folio". In a rage Sir
Harry threw the animal on the floor. At this dis-
respect shown to her squirrel, Lady Willit called Sir
Harry "a sower Pedant without good Nature or good

Manners". Sir Harry now really forgot himself, and
he "threw down the table before him and Kicked the
Book round the Room". But at once he was sorry:
" 'Lord, Madam,' said he, 'why did you run into such
Expressions? I was', said he, 'in the highest Delight
with that Author when you clapp'd your Squirrel
upon my Book'; and smiling upon Recollection, 'I
have a great Respect for your Favourite, and pray
let us all be Friends' ".

This touching apology made no impression on his
agitated lady. Her living favourite had been roughly
handled, and to her his loved folio was a dead thing.
She unfortunately conceived the idea of keeping him,
as he has so far humbled himself, "under for ever".
After telling him in vigorous language that she
despised him, she rushed from the room, and when
Sir Harry followed her to her bedchamber he found
her "prostrate upon the Bed, tearing her Hair, and
naming Twenty Coxcombs who would have used her
otherwise". Sir Harry was now so provoked that "he
forbore nothing but beating her", and the servants
listened "while the best Man and Woman, the best
Master and Mistress, defamed each other in a Way
that is not to be repeated even in Billingsgate" (*Tatler*,
79). The quarrel had become irreconcilable, and an
immediate separation followed. Many writers might
have made us smile at the manners of the pedant and
the hoyden of the day; Steele can stir our sympathy
equally for the raw girl, married almost certainly for
the benefit of her family's property, and for Sir Harry,

tied to a woman to whom his "high Delight" in the folio was incomprehensible.

But although literary success and genuine happiness came to Steele through his peculiar gifts of mind and heart, more serious trouble than the danger of empty-ing his pockets at the appeal of beggars, could never be far from a man of his temperament. Berkeley noticed that Steele's benevolence was directed to-wards "mankind"; but he could not notice, in their one meeting, a certain toughness of fibre in Steele's character. Whenever Steele believed that a duty to the public was involved, he became the persistent champion of a succession of unpopular causes, and, in their defence, showed a determination and staying-power for which his contemporaries did not give him credit; and which could, in fact, hardly be estimated until his life was looked at as a whole. It is interesting to find from the *Oxford English Dictionary* that Steele was apparently the first writer to use the phrase, "public spirit" in the modern sense.[1] In *Tatler* 183 he writes: "However general Custom may hurry us away in the Stream of a Common Error, there is no Evil, no Crime, so great as that of being cold in Matters which relate to the common Good." Even philosophers were not to be excused from action. "It is the Duty of all", he says, "who make Philosophy the Entertainment of their Lives, to turn their Thoughts to practical Schemes for the Good of

[1] Steele, in the first number of the *Englishman* (1714), says that his object is "to rouze in this country that lost thing called Publick Spirit".

Society and not to pass away their Time in fruitless Searches, which tend rather to the Ostentation of Knowledge, than the Service of Life" (*Tatler*, 261).

It is the reality of this conviction that makes him throughout the *Tatler* and *Spectator* keep up such a constant fire of attack on injustice and cruelty. On the subject of sport, so sacred to his countrymen in high places, he wrote in a way that not even in the twentieth century would be acceptable. "When", he says, "any of these Ends are not served"—and he has particularized slaughter for our safety, convenience, or nourishment—"in the Destruction of a living Creature, I cannot but pronounce it a great Piece of Cruelty, if not a kind of Murder" (*Tatler*, 134).

Steele, writing only a few years after Locke's death, was not alone in his distress at the cruelty thought necessary in the making of scholars, and his papers on the subject of flogging must have had many sympathizers. He is, however, not content to appeal to the simple humanity of the question, but attacks the "Stupidity" of schoolmasters. In *Spectator* 157 he says: "It happens, I doubt not, more than once in a Year, that a Lad is chastised for a Blockhead, when it is good Apprehension that makes him incapable of knowing what his Teacher means." Nor does he spare the products of this system—the educated gentleman of his day. He thinks that "to be bred like a Gentleman and punished like a Malefactor, must, as we see it does, produce that illiberal Sauciness which we sometimes see in Men of Letters".

And he adds that it is to this "dreadful Practice" that we may attribute "a certain Hardness and Ferocity which some Men tho' liberally educated, carry about with them in all their Behaviour" (*Tatler*, 134).

The strength of Steele's feelings on social questions disturbed the tone of urbanity that characterized the *Tatler*. He writes that: "Fortune has taken up all our Minds and, as I have often complained, Poverty and Riches stand in our Imagination in the place of Guilt and Innocence." And he adds, "It is not allowed me to speak of Luxury and Folly with the severe Spirit they deserve" (*Tatler*, 271).

The end of the *Tatler* was so sudden that it came even to Addison as a surprise. Steele in the last number gives his own reasons for dropping it abruptly. His anonymity could be no longer maintained, and the public knew that the Mr. Bickerstaffe who censured them so severely was the same Dick Steele, the contrast between whose ideal in the *Christian Hero* (1701) and his own faulty life they had never forgotten or forgiven. But more than this, during the years of the publication of both the *Tatler* and *Spectator*, Steele's political opinions showed themselves more and more clearly. "What I find", he says in that last number of the *Tatler*, "the least excusable Part of all this Work is, that I have, in some Places in it touched upon Matters which concern both Church and State. All I shall say, for this is, That the Points I alluded to are such as concerned every Christian and Freeholder in England: and I could not be cold enough to conceal my Opinion on Subjects which related to either of those Characters."

At first in the *Spectator* it seemed as if Steele had learnt his lesson and would accept the idea that the paper was to be more strictly impartial than the *Tatler* had been. "I never", Addison writes in its first number, "espoused any Party with Violence, and am resolved to observe an exact Neutrality between the Whigs and Tories, unless I shall be forced to declare myself by the Hostilities of either side."

Steele's notions, however, of what constituted hostilities had to be counted with, and he had evidently declared himself too plainly for the *Spectator's* reputation for impartiality, when on July 1, 1712, Swift writes of him to Stella: "I believe he will very soon lose his employment, for he has been mighty impertinent of late in his Spectators; and I will never offer a word in his behalf."

There can be little doubt that it was Steele's growing conviction that in these last years of Queen Anne's reign the Protestant succession was in real danger, which led to his breaking his connection with the *Spectator* at the end of Vol. VII. Addison helped at first with Steele's new venture, the *Guardian*; but their real co-operation was over. Steele, speaking of party politics in the first number of the *Guardian*, says, "As to these Matters I shall be Impartial"; but he adds characteristically, "tho' I cannot be Neuter". He describes himself "as past the Regards of this

Life", and as having "nothing to manage with any Person or Party, but to deliver my self as becomes an Old Man with one Foot in the Grave". But by April this old gentleman with "one Foot in the Grave" and who thinks of himself as "passing to Eternity" is engaged in a lively quarrel with the *Examiner* over an attack that paper made (No. 241) on Lady Charlotte Finch. Libellers were always anathema to Steele. In *Tatler* 92 he warns "these Children of Infamy" that it will be useless for them to hope to escape him, by publishing "their Works under feigned Names or under none at all, for I am so perfectly well acquainted with the Styles of all my Contemporaries that I shall not fail of doing them Justice with their proper Names, and at their full length". If, he says in the same essay, a great name is libelled, "we should run on such an Occasion (as if a publick Building was on Fire) to their Relief".

To defend Lady Charlotte, Steele ran "as if a public Building were on Fire". The occasion the *Examiner* chose for its attack was when Lady Charlotte's father, Lord Nottingham, joined the Whigs. On April 28, 1713, in the *Guardian* (No. 41), Steele writes: "The *Examiner* ends his Discourse of Friday the 24th Instant with these Words, 'No sooner was D—— among the Whigs and confirmed past retrieving, but Lady Char——te is taken Knotting in St. James's Chappel during Divine Service in the immediate Presence both of God and Her Majesty, who were affronted together'." Steele fiercely resented this attack on a father through his daughter. "Of what Temper", he writes, "can this Man be made that could have no Sense of the Pangs of a young Lady to be barely mentioned in a Publick Paper?" He goes on to call the writer of the article "a fawning Miscreant" and a "Wretch, as dull as he is wicked". "In the immediate Presence of God and her Majesty", he quotes, and adds scornfully, "It is very visible which of these Powers (that he has put together) he is the more fearful of offending".[1] Steele's hard hitting had an effect; a letter was published in the *Examiner* which stated: "She knotted, it is true, in the Chapel, upon some Wednesday in Lent, but it was before Divine Service began, and out of pure Inadvertency." This letter was followed by something in the nature of an apology from the editor, who says: "Nothing but an entire submission to another Lady, as irresistible as Lady Ch——e, could have betray'd me into that Severity which has since cost me more Concern than it has the injur'd fair one."[2]

For the moment Steele had won, but the *Guardian* continued to give offence, and on October 1st it ceased publication. Addison, in a much quoted passage, wrote a few weeks later: "I am in a thousand troubles for poor Dick, and wish that his zeal for the public may not be ruinous to himself, but he has sent me word that he has determined to go on, and that any advice I can give him in this particular will have no weight with him." It is little wonder that the

[1] *Guardian*, 41.   [2] *Examiner*, 48.

SIR RICHARD STEELE
(From the mezzotint by J. Simon, after Sir Godfrey Kneller)

accumulated feelings of the political enemies of the
irrepressible Steele were strong; for whether in the
character of the loved old Bickerstaffe, the urbane
impartial *Spectator*, or of Nestor Ironside, the cheerful
old gentleman with "one foot in the grave", or the
frank "Patriot" of the Englishman,[1] he had given
them little peace.

On March 18, 1714, a motion to expel Steele from
the House of Commons, to which he had been elected
for Stockbridge in the preceding August, was introduced on the ground that in his *Crisis* (January
1713) he had maliciously insinuated "that the Protestant succession in the House of Hanover is in danger
under her Majesty's administration".

The young Lord Finch, Lady Charlotte's brother,
rose to make his maiden speech in defence of his
sister's champion. "But bashfulness overcame him;
and after a few confused sentences he sat down,
crying out as he did so, 'It is strange I cannot speak
for this man, though I would readily fight for him!'
Upon this such cheering rang through the House that
suddenly the young lord took heart, rose again, and
made the first of a long series of telling and able
speeches."[2] In spite of the fact that not only Lord
Finch, but the Whigs as a whole, rallied to his support, Steele was expelled by a majority of nearly a
hundred, in a house of four hundred members. In his
"Apology for Himself and his Writings", written just

[1] Aitken, *Life of Richard Steele*, Vol. I, p. 406.
[2] John Forster, *Historical and Biographical Essays*, Vol. II, p. 195.

after his expulsion, Steele, usually only too modest, speaks of himself as "one who with Poverty and Disgrace staring in his Face", did what he could "to rouse his Country out of a Lethargy", and that "from the irresistible Force of the Love he bears Mankind".

It is this Steele, the Steele whose "irresistible love of mankind" gave purpose and direction to a life which he described as "at its best but pardonable" (*Tatler*, 271), who since the days of the *Christian Hero* had regarded "the reasonable Service of Women" as one of his chief objects. When in *Tatler* 128 he wrote that he intended to "serve them to his last drop of Ink", it was not the gallant who wrote, but a man who, when he believed that the public good was at stake, again and again chose to throw away the popularity which his gay gifts made it so easy for him to win. It was his obstinacy in well-doing that enabled him in a few years to make a real impression on the accepted fashion of treating with contemptuous badinage the legal and educational position of women.

Even Steele's lighter touches on the subject of women are a relief from those of his contemporaries, because of the underlying assumption that folly is not confined to one sex, and his equal readiness to laugh, whether it is a man or a woman who is guilty of it. Jenny Simper writes: "I am a young Woman and have my Fortune to make, for which Reason I come constantly to Church to hear Divine Service and make Conquests." She complains that, owing to the heavy

decoration of the Church at Christmas time, "I have
not seen the young Baronet I dress at these three
Weeks" (*Spectator*, 282). But the young beau who is
anxious to be regarded as a man of the world is not
let off, and Steele tells us of Tom Springly, "who
t'other Day pretended to go to an Assignment with a
Married Woman at Rosamond's Pond, and was seen
soon after reading the Responses with great Gravity
at six a clock Prayers" (*Tatler*, 231). "In their common
Behaviour" he finds women "of ordinary Genius are
not more trivial than the Common Rate of Men; and
in my Opinion, the Playing of a Fan is every whit as
good an Entertainment as the beating of a Snuff box"
(*Tatler*, 172). If women's vanity in their dress is absurd,
he points out that there are also men who are exactly
in the "like Condition to be regarded for a well tied
Cravat, an Hat cocked with an unusual Briskness"
(*Spectator*, 38). On the other hand, a letter which he
inserts from a girl of nineteen shows how well he
understood one of the troubles of a rational young
woman of his and of a much later day. "Our House",
she writes, "is frequented by Men of Sense, and I love
to ask Questions when I fall into such Conversation,
but I am cut short with something or other about my
bright Eyes. There is, Sir, a Language particular for
talking to Women; and none but those of the very
first good Breeding (who are very few and who
seldom come into my way) can speak to us without
regard to our Sex" (*Spectator*, 534). In this matter
Steele himself showed the "first good breeding"; he

answered the questions of women with the same seriousness with which he answered the questions of men, and when Swift writes in his *Journal* to Stella on February 8, 1712, "I will not meddle with the Spectator. Let him fair sex it to the world's end", it may well be that what was objected to was not Steele's constant reference to the "fair sex", but his attitude towards the whole subject.

To understand how new Steele's attitude was, we need not turn to the dreary and not always decent pleasantries of the lesser wits. We have only to compare Steele's writing on women, in the *Tatler* and *Spectator*, with Addison's. Addison, when he noticed that Lord Halifax, in his *Advice to a Daughter*, says nothing on the subject of jealousy, addresses himself to "my Fair Correspondents who desire to live well with a jealous Husband". His advice is that if a woman has a jealous husband whose "Temper be Grave or Sullen, you must not be too much pleased with a Jest, or transported with any thing that is gay or diverting. If his Beauty be none of the best, you must be a profest Admirer of Prudence, or any other Quality he is master of, or at least vain enough to think he is" (*Spectator*, 171). Again in *Spectator* 89 Addison warns the women, whom he calls "Demurrers", not to lose their suitors by a pretended indifference. But this needed careful management, for "a Retreat from the first Approaches of a Lover" is, he admits, "both fashionable and graceful", and "a virtuous Woman should reject the first Offer of Marriage, as a good Man does that of a Bishoprick; but I would advise neither the one nor the other to persist in refusing what they secretly approve".

In the eighth volume of the *Spectator*, for which Addison was alone responsible, the most serious paper on the subject is a plea to women to practise the art of embroidery. While they are thus occupied, the writer says that they will not gossip and "their Neighbours will be allowed to be the Fathers of their own Children". He describes the delight of the fair sex, "whom their native Modesty, and the Tenderness of Men towards them, exempts from Publick Business", in passing their time "in imitating Fruits and Flowers." "How pleasing", he adds, "is the Amusement of walking among the Shades and Groves planted by themselves, in surveying Heroes slain by their Needle, or little Cupids which they have brought into the World without Pain" (*Spectator*, 606).

It had always appeared to Steele that "to manage well a Great Family, is as worthy an Instance of Capacity, as to execute a great Employment" (*Tatler*, 172). The utter neglect of women's education was never far from his thoughts. He did not exaggerate when he spoke (*Tatler*, 61) of an "unaccountable wild Method in the Education of the better half of the World, the Women". Defoe, only twelve years before the *Tatler* appeared, had written, in his *Essay on Projects on an Academy for Women*: "Their Youth is spent," he says, "to teach them to stitch and sew or make baubles. They are taught to read indeed, and perhaps to write their names or so, and that is the height of a woman's education."

A common opinion at that time, and one that Steele opposes, was that girls, through social visiting in early childhood, had a great advantage over boys. The unknown author of a *Defence of the Female Sex* (so long thought to be by Mary Astell), takes this view. She speaks of the improving effect on little girls of making and receiving visits with their mothers. This, she writes,[1] "gives them betimes the opportunity of imitating, conversing with, and knowing the manner, and address of elder Persons. These I take it to be the two Reasons why a girl of Fifteen is reckon'd as ripe as a Boy of One and Twenty." A father writes to Mr. Bickerstaffe for advice. He wants his daughter, who is "about nine years of age", to go to boarding-school. The girl's mother opposes this, not on the ground of her youth, but because "she is too much a Woman, and understands the Formalities of Visiting, and a Tea-Table so very nicely, that none, tho' much older, can exceed her" (*Tatler*, 141).

Steele thought that to learn from your mother up to the age of nine the formalities of the tea-table and to practise them for ever after was not enough to satisfy the needs of the mind and body of a growing girl. He has looked around him and he tells us (*Tatler*, 248): "I could name you twenty Families where all the Girls hear of in this Life is that it is time to rise and to come to Dinner; as if they were so insignificant

---

[1] *Essay in Defence of the Female Sex*, p. 57.

as to be wholly provided for when they are fed and Cloathed." And he adds: "It is with great Indignation that I see such Crowds of the Female World lost to human Society, and condemned to a Laziness which makes Life pass away with less Relish than in the hardest Labour."

Girls, in Steele's day, had to forgo not only knowledge, but many innocent pleasures. Steele's genuine delight at the unconventionality of a young lady whom he met "mounted on a Pad [i.e. a pony] in Enfield Chase" is infectious. "It may perhaps", he writes, "appear ridiculous" that she had not been "out of my Head or, for aught I know, my Heart, ever since". "To be well diverted", he tells the parents of girls, "is the safest Guard to Innocence; and methinks it should be one of the first things to be regarded among people of Condition, to find out proper Amusement for Young Ladies." If the healthy exercise of riding could be revived among them, "this would lay up the best Portion they could bring into a Family, a good Stock of Health, to transmit to their Posterity".

It is, however, the effect on married life of the enforced idleness and utter ignorance of the girls of his own class, that troubles him most. "Were the general Turn of Women's Education", he wrote, "of another kind than it is at present, we should want one another for more Reasons than we do as the World now goes" (*Tatler*, 248). And what he speaks of as "the unnatural Marriages which happen every Day" would be prevented. Girls, he complained, when they

read at all, read little but gay romances, and thought
of themselves as "Goddesses, Nymphs and Shepherd-
esses"; while young men, during courtship, treated
them as if they were to "inhabit the happy Fields of
Arcadia, rather then be Wives and Mothers in old
England". Steele thought that a lover should let his
mistress know "in a Billet" that he had noticed and
been captivated by "her Piety to her Parents, her
Gentleness of Behaviour, her prudent Economy with
respect to her own little Affairs in a Virgin Condition" (*Tatler*, 139). And when giving his advice to a
lady (*Tatler*, 247) on love, he says: "In a word, Madam,
if you would judge aright in love, you must look upon
it as a case of friendship." But marriage might be in
Steele's view more than a "case of friendship". In
Tatler 150 a correspondent writes of "those" who
"arrive within few Months at a Pitch of Benevolence
and Affection, of which the most perfect Friendship
is but a faint Resemblance", and in *Spectator* 490 he
speaks of the kind of wife who "brings Happiness
unknown to Friendship itself".

Another, and an even more serious cause of unhappiness in marriage, was the question of jointures
and settlements, and on this point Steele undertook
the unpopular task of attacking the deep-rooted and
respected customs of his class and country. In *Tatler*
199 he writes: "I am the more serious, large and particular on this subject, because my Lucubrations,
designed for the Encouragement of Virtue cannot
have the desired Success as long as this Incumbrance

of Settlements continues upon Matrimony." "The World", he says, "is mercenary even to the buying and selling of our very Persons", and "young Women, tho' they have never so great Attractions from Nature, are never the nearer being happily disposed of in Marriage" (*Spectator*, 155). On the other hand, those whose settlements and jointures had been satisfactorily arranged by their elders, often found themselves indifferent or even hateful to each other, in a relationship which Steele describes as "Bargains to cohabit" (*Tatler*, 149), and again he speaks of the "Men of Wit and Pleasure of the Age" who have introduced "separate Beds, silent Tables, and solitary Homes" (*Tatler*, 159).

It took some courage to treat the position of married women with seriousness, but unmarried women, except by a few religious writers, were everywhere regarded as the butt of the wits. Steele, who had complained in a general way that it was the custom to treat poverty, not as a misfortune but as a crime, knew that for women it meant that to be "disposed of" in marriage "was impossible", and that their position as spinsters was intolerable. Why, he asks, shall it not be open to them "to go into a Way of Trade for their Maintenance"? "But", he says, "their very Excellencies and personal Perfections shall be a Disadvantage to them, and subject them to be treated as if they stood there to sell their Persons to Prostitution." He publishes a letter from a woman who keeps a coffee-house, and who complains that half a dozen

men "loll at the Bar, staring just in my Face, ready
to interpret my Looks and Gestures according to
their own imaginations". This representation Steele
speaks of as "just", and he quotes from other letters
on the same subject. "They tell me", he writes, "that
a young Fop cannot buy a Pair of Gloves, but he
is at the same Time straining for some ingenious
Ribaldry to say to the young Woman who helps
them on." If, Steele argues, men had weighed the
difficulties that meet women who desire to make an
honest livelihood, "it would be as much Impertinence
to go into a Shop of one of these young Women without buying, as into that of any other Trader" (*Spectator*, 155).

Plain speaking on the social position of women, if
the writer took the unpopular side, was not more
welcome in the eighteenth century than at any other
date. "Your Papers", a correspondent writes, in
Spectator 276, "which regard the fallen Part of the fair
Sex are, I think, written with an indelicacy which
makes them unworthy to be inserted in the Writings
of a Moralist who knows the World. . . ." Some
months before, in *Spectator* 182, Steele had published
a letter that begins:

"MR. SPECTATOR,

    "It is wonderful to me that among the many
Enormities which you have treated of you have not
mentioned that of Wenching, and particularly the
insnaring Part."

His correspondent tells him that she was one of those who, when she was deserted, had "so much Indignation and Resolution as not to go upon the Town, as the Phrase is, but took to work for my Living in an obscure Place". Now that she has a business of her own, she complains that "a Sett of idle Fellows about this Town" are constantly sending messages and making appointments with "little raw unthinking Girls" (*Spectator*, 266). Steele, when he writes in the same number of the women of the town, pleads that they should not be "huddled in the Common Word due to the worst of Women". "The compassionate Case of very many is that they are taken into such Hands without the least Suspicion, previous Temptation, or Admonition, to what Place they are going." Again, in *Spectator* 274, he says: "Regard is to be had to their Circumstances when they fell, to the uneasy Perplexity under which they lived under senseless and severe Parents, and the Importunity of Poverty, to the Violence of Passion in its Beginning well grounded."

He writes, in *Tatler* 84: "I have received a Letter subscribed A.B. wherein it has been represented to me as an Enormity, that there are more than ordinary Crowds of Women at the Old Bailey when a Rape is to be tried." Steele's answer is: "I can't tell who are so much concerned in that Part of the Law as the Sex he mentions, they being the only Persons liable to such Insults." And he tells us that "several eminent Ladies appeared lately at the Court of Justice on such an Occasion and with great Patience and Attention staid the whole Trials of two Persons for the abovesaid Crime. The Law to me indeed seems a little defective in this Point; and it is a very great Hardship, that this Crime, which is committed by Men only, should have Men only on their Jury."

When the *Tatler* and the *Spectator* are read to-day it is generally for the sake of the few gems of literature that Steele and Addison produced at their best; or because in them the curious find a record of manners and habits of thought that have gone from modern life. That these volumes contain something more than this is due to a quality of Steele's character that annoyed his contemporaries, because it made him give, a century and a half before the reform movements of the nineteenth century, constant and courageous expression to the wrongs and the hopes of humble people; and because his point of view on every question was, as he says of himself in *Tatler* 167, that of a man who looked "upon the Distinctions amongst Men to be merely scenical".

INDEX

For Product Safety Concerns and Information please contact our EU
representative GPSR@taylorandfrancis.com
Taylor & Francis Verlag GmbH, Kaufingerstraße 24, 80331 München, Germany

www.ingramcontent.com/pod-product-compliance
Lightning Source LLC
Chambersburg PA
CBHW062020270326
41929CB00014B/2268

* 9 7 8 1 0 3 2 9 0 7 4 5 1 *